W9-BVI-279

Best of the Best

the best recipes from the **25** best cookbooks of the year

from the editors of
FOOD & WINE

FOOD & WINE BEST OF THE BEST VOL. 10
EDITOR **Kate Heddings**
ART DIRECTOR **Patricia Sanchez**
DESIGNER **Nancy Blumberg**
FEATURES EDITOR **Michelle Shih**
SENIOR EDITOR **Zoe Singer**
ASSISTANT FOOD EDITOR **Melissa Rubel**
COPY EDITOR **Wendy G. Ramunno**
PRODUCTION MANAGER **Matt Carson**
REPORTERS **Kristin Donnelly, Emily Kaiser, Megan Krigbaum, Jen Murphy, Stacey Nield, Kelly Snowden, Jessica Tzerman, Emery Van Hook**

FOOD & WINE MAGAZINE
EDITOR IN CHIEF **Dana Cowin**
CREATIVE DIRECTOR **Stephen Scoble**
MANAGING EDITOR **Mary Ellen Ward**
EXECUTIVE EDITOR **Pamela Kaufman**
EXECUTIVE FOOD EDITOR **Tina Ujlaki**
ART DIRECTOR **Patricia Sanchez**

AMERICAN EXPRESS PUBLISHING CORPORATION
PRESIDENT/C.E.O. **Ed Kelly**
SENIOR VICE PRESIDENT, CHIEF MARKETING OFFICER **Mark V. Stanich**
C.F.O./S.V.P./CORPORATE DEVELOPMENT & OPERATIONS **Paul B. Francis**
VICE PRESIDENT, BOOKS AND PRODUCTS **Marshall Corey**
PRODUCTION DIRECTOR **Rosalie Abatemarco Samat**
CORPORATE PRODUCTION MANAGER **Stuart N. Handelman**
SENIOR MARKETING MANAGER **Bruce Spanier**
ASSISTANT MARKETING MANAGER **Sarah Ross**
DIRECTOR OF FULFILLMENT **Phil Black**
BUSINESS MANAGER **Thomas Noonan**

COVER
PHOTOGRAPH James Baigrie
FOOD STYLING Alison Attenborough
PROP STYLING Dani Fisher
FLAP PHOTOGRAPHS
DANA COWIN PORTRAIT Andrew French
KATE HEDDINGS PORTRAIT Andrew French

Best of the Best

the best recipes from the **25** best cookbooks of the year

FOOD&WINE
BOOKS

American Express Publishing Corporation, New York

THE New Greek Cuisine

Featuring 150 Recipes from Jim Botsacos, the Chef of New York's Acclaimed Molyvos Restaurant

Jim Botsacos with Judith Choate

BRAISE

A Journey Through International Cuisine

DANIEL BOULUD AND MELISSA CLARK

THE CAKE BOOK

TISH BOYLE · PHOTOGRAPHY BY JOHN UHER

THE RED CAT COOKBOOK

130 RECIPES FROM NEW YORK'S FAVORITE NEIGHBORHOOD RESTAURANT

JIMMY BRADLEY & ANDREW FRIEDMAN

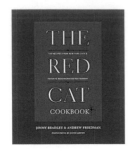

HEIRLOOM BAKING WITH THE BRASS SISTERS

More than 100 Years of Recipes Discovered from Family Cookbooks, Original Journals, Scraps of Paper, & Grandmother's Kitchen

MARILYNN BRASS & SHEILA BRASS · Photographs by ANDY RYAN

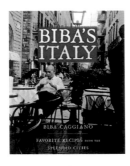

BIBA'S ITALY

BIBA CAGGIANO

FAVORITE RECIPES FROM THE SPLENDID CITIES

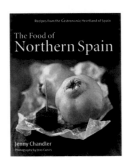

Recipes from the Gastronomic Heartland of Spain

The Food of Northern Spain

Jenny Chandler

Photography by Jean Cazals

GIADA DE LAURENTIIS author of the bestselling everyday italian

giada's family dinners

more than 1,000 fresh recipes, tips, and photos for beginning cooks

food network kitchens

HOW TO BOIL WATER

life beyond takeout

barefoot contessa at home

everyday recipes you'll make over and over again

ina garten

A LIGURIAN KITCHEN

RECIPES AND TALES from THE ITALIAN RIVIERA

LAURA GIANNATEMPO

photographs by MICHAEL PIAZZA

On Top of Spaghetti...

...Macaroni, Linguine, Penne, and Pasta of Every Kind

Johanne Killeen and George Germon

stonewall kitchen favorites

DELICIOUS RECIPES TO SHARE WITH FAMILY AND FRIENDS EVERY DAY

jonathan king, jim stott, and kathy gunst

FOREWORD BY ina garten

THE LEE BROS. SOUTHERN COOKBOOK

MATT LEE and TED LEE

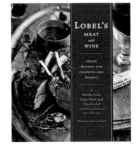

LOBEL'S MEAT and WINE

GREAT RECIPES FOR COOKING AND PAIRING

Stanley, Leon, Evan, Mark, and David Lobel

Photographs by Louis Wallach

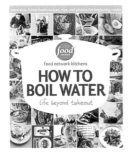

JAMIE OLIVER jamie's italy

AUTHOR OF The Naked Chef

Cindy Pawlcyn with Pablo Jacinto & Erasto Jacinto

Big Small Plates

The Good Home Cookbook

MORE THAN 1000 CLASSIC AMERICAN RECIPES

Tested in home kitchens across America!

Edited by Richard J. Perry

THE ESSENCE OF CHOCOLATE

JOHN SCHARFFENBERGER and ROBERT STEINBERG

¡BAJA! COOKING ON THE EDGE

DEBORAH M. SCHNEIDER

PHOTOGRAPHS BY MAREN CARUSO

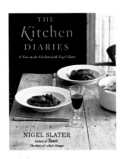

THE Kitchen DIARIES

A Year in the Kitchen with Nigel Slater

NIGEL SLATER

Author of Toast: The Story of a Boy's Hunger

SPICE

Flavors of the Eastern Mediterranean

ANA SORTUN CHEF, Oleana

PHOTOGRAPHY BY SUSIE CUSHNER

SPARKS IN THE KITCHEN

A deliciously creative cookbook by a talented chef who applies her professional know-how to home cooking and makes every dish sparkle

KATY SPARKS with ANDREA STRONG

"Spice: simply one of the most definitive reads I've had this year."—MARIO BATALI

Cucina of Le Marche FABIO TRABOCCHI with PETER KAMINSKY

A Chef's Treasury of Recipes from Italy's Last Culinary Frontier

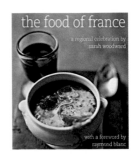

the food of france

a regional celebration by sarah woodward

with a foreword by raymond blanc

Contents

Each chapter highlights the best recipes from one of the year's best books.

Recipe titles in **bold** are brand-new dishes appearing exclusively in *Best of the Best*.

Contents

Recipes

Poultry

Meat

Vegetables & Sides

Desserts

Foreword

Producing *Best of the Best* gives us a terrific opportunity for cookbook trend spotting. In the past year, for instance, we saw fewer chef cookbooks featuring complicated recipes, and more books highlighting approachable, homestyle dishes. Two standout examples are Daniel Boulud's luscious *Braise*, which is packed with slow-cooked dishes like succulent Beef Short Ribs with Daikon Radish, and Ana Sortun's *Spice,* which has a delicious (and unexpected) recipe for hummus made with parsnips.

We were also delighted to see more cookbooks championing classic American dishes. *The Good Home Cookbook* offers more than 1,000 recipes culled from old cookbooks and tested by hundreds of home cooks around the U.S.; Chicken Chili Verde and German Pancakes are part of the eclectic and irresistible mix. And for *Heirloom Baking,* Marilynn and Sheila Brass searched through their own cherished collection of books and recipe boxes to compile an assortment that includes an incredible Banana Cream Pie.

But by far the biggest swell in the market continues to be cookbooks from TV stars like Giada De Laurentiis and Jamie Oliver, who impress us with their easy, delightful recipes (we adored Jamie's Spaghetti Fritters). Even the Food Network Kitchens have a book this year—an excellent starter book called *How To Boil Water* that belongs on every new cook's shelf.

No matter the trend, each of these books has proven itself to be one of the best of 2006, with recipes that not only taste terrific but work fabulously well. As a *Best of the Best* bonus, many of the authors have given us a special never-before-published recipe; we urge you to try Jimmy Bradley's Scallop Fritters and the Brass sisters' Toasted-Almond Butter Cookies. We're proud to include them in our annual compendium.

Editor in Chief
FOOD & WINE MAGAZINE

Editor FOOD & WINE COOKBOOKS

Steamed Mediterranean Mussels with
Cinnamon Basil, Ouzo, and Feta Cheese, p. 14

The New Greek Cuisine

By Jim Botsacos with Judith Choate

In his first cookbook, Jim Botsacos, chef at Manhattan's Molyvos and Abboccato restaurants, adds his own creative touch to classic Greek dishes. "I found that if I took some additional steps in putting traditional recipes together, I could raise the intensity of the essence of the dish," he says. For instance, simple steamed mussels get pumped up with cinnamon basil, ouzo and feta cheese, along with homemade clam broth. The book showcases Botsacos's talent as a chef, as well as his ability to keep recipes simple and approachable.

Published by Broadway Books, $29.95.
Find more recipes by Jim Botsacos at foodandwine.com/botsacos

Steamed Mediterranean Mussels with Cinnamon Basil, Ouzo, and Feta Cheese

Editor's Note

Aleppo is a dried, lightly salted Turkish chile pepper used frequently in Greek cuisine. It has subtle heat and a rich, smoky taste. You can substitute other red chile flakes, or order Aleppo from Penzeys Spices (penzeys.com).

If you can find them, use cultivated Mediterranean mussels that are grown in California or Washington State. They have a thin shell and plump, juicy meat. If you can't find them, try for Prince Edward Island mussels, which are almost as good. I love the scent of the cinnamon basil, but you can use absolutely any herb that pleases you. Whatever you do, however, have plenty of crusty bread to sop up the delicious broth.

SERVES 6

- ¼ cup olive oil
- 2 garlic cloves, sliced

Pinch of Aleppo pepper

- 1 medium tomato, peeled, seeded, and chopped (see Note, page 18)
- ½ cup ouzo
- 2 cups Clam Broth (recipe follows)
- 2 tablespoons chopped fresh cinnamon basil
- 90 mussels, scrubbed and debearded

Grated zest of 1 lemon

- ½ cup diced feta cheese

Coarse salt and freshly ground pepper

- 2 tablespoons extra virgin olive oil

1. Preheat the broiler.

2. Heat the olive oil in a sauteuse or large shallow pan over medium-high heat. Add the garlic and cook for about 2 minutes, or just until fragrant. Add the Aleppo pepper, stirring to blend. Stir in the tomato and cook for 1 minute. Remove from the heat and add the ouzo. Using a long kitchen match, carefully ignite the alcohol and then let the flames subside. Return to medium-high heat and cook for 2 minutes. Add the broth and ¼ of the basil along with the mussels, cover, and steam for 4 to 5 minutes, shaking the pan from time to time to allow the mussels to cook evenly. When all of the mussels have opened, transfer them to a large, flat, ovenproof serving dish, placing them, top shell toward the outside, in a concentric circle. Discard any mussels that have not opened.

3. Add the lemon zest and half of the feta to the sauce. Season with salt and pepper and add the remaining basil. Spoon the sauce over the mussels. Sprinkle the mussel meat with the remaining feta. Drizzle olive oil over all and broil for 2 minutes, or just until the cheese has softened. Serve immediately.

Clam Broth

MAKES ABOUT 2½ QUARTS

- 12 large chowder clams
- 2 garlic cloves, sliced
- 2 fresh parsley stems
- 1 bay leaf
- ½ cup dry white wine

1. Using a kitchen scrub pad (such as a Dobie pad), vigorously wash the clams under cold running water. Place in a large bowl of cold water and swish the water to dislodge any remaining debris. Pour off the water and rinse the clams 2 or 3 more times, or until the water is perfectly clear.

2. Combine the garlic, parsley, and bay leaf in a large shallow nonreactive saucepan over medium heat. Add the wine and bring to a boil. Boil for about 5 minutes, or until reduced by half. Add 2 quarts water and bring to a simmer. Put the clams into the broth, cover, and raise the heat. Bring to a low simmer and cook for about 15 minutes, or until the clams have opened and a fragrant broth has formed. Turn off the heat and steep for 5 minutes.

3. Remove from the heat and drain well through a fine sieve, discarding the solids. Taste the broth. If too strongly flavored for your taste, add water, ¼ cup at a time. Place in an ice bath to cool quickly.

4. Store, covered and refrigerated, for up to 1 week or frozen for up to 3 weeks.

Botsacos on Clam Juice

Bottled clam juice can be used in place of homemade clam broth, but you may have to dilute it. Pour the juice into a saucepan and warm it; taste and add a little water if the flavor is too strong.

Shrimp Saganaki with Tomato and Feta

The term *saganaki* actually refers to the metal skillet-like pan with two handles in which various dishes, including the classic Greek fried cheese dish, are traditionally served. The term is also used to describe dishes incorporating tomatoes, onions, and feta cheese prepared in a baking pan. This dish is easy to prepare and makes a sensational presentation served in the traditional pan. If you don't have the traditional pan, use an attractive baking dish. I use both fresh and canned tomatoes for their difference in texture and acidity.

SERVES 6

¼ cup extra virgin olive oil, plus oil for drizzling

½ cup finely diced onion

Coarse salt and freshly ground pepper

3 garlic cloves, minced

1 teaspoon dried Greek oregano, plus oregano for sprinkling

1 cup diced peeled, seeded ripe tomatoes (see Note, page 18)

¼ cup dry white wine

One 28-ounce can chopped tomatoes with juice

¼ cup chopped fresh flat-leaf parsley

1½ pounds medium shrimp, peeled and deveined, tails left on

¾ cup diced feta cheese

1. Preheat the oven to 450°F.

2. Heat ¼ cup oil in a large sauté pan over medium heat. Add the onion along with a pinch of salt. Cover and cook, stirring occasionally, for 8 minutes, or until soft and translucent. Add the garlic and sauté for another minute. Stir in the oregano along with a pinch of salt. Add the diced tomatoes and the wine and bring to a simmer. Simmer for 3 minutes.

3. Stir in the canned tomatoes with their juice, raise the heat to medium-high, and again bring to a simmer. Simmer for about 6 minutes, or until the sauce has thickened slightly. Fold in the parsley and season with salt and pepper to taste, noting that the feta will add some saltiness.

4. Spoon just enough tomato sauce into the bottom of a saganaki pan (or a 9 x 14-inch glass baking dish) to cover. Working from the outside in, make 3 concentric circles of shrimp. (If using a baking pan, begin placing the shrimp, three at a time, tail-to-head, in neat rows across the dish, with the tails all facing in the same direction and just barely touching. Add the remaining shrimp in overlapping rows of 3, shingle fashion, until the dish is filled. You should have 3 rows of 13 to 15 shrimp each.) Season the shrimp with salt and pepper to taste and then spoon the remaining tomato sauce over the top. Sprinkle the feta cheese over the top, drizzle with olive oil, and sprinkle with oregano.

5. Bake in the middle of the preheated oven for 20 minutes, or until very hot and bubbling with golden brown cheese.

NOTE To peel tomatoes, bring a pot of water to a boil. Core and lightly score the tomato skin in quarters. Place the scored tomato in the boiling water for 30 seconds. Immediately remove and place the tomato in ice water to chill. Remove from the ice water and, using a paring knife, carefully pull off the skin. Once peeled, the tomato can be used in any recipe calling for cored, peeled tomatoes.

Grilled Lamb Chops with Ionian Garlic Sauce

SERVES 6

1½ cups extra virgin olive oil

Juice of 1 lemon

2 tablespoons chopped garlic

1 tablespoon dried Greek oregano

1½ teaspoons dried Greek savory

Coarse salt and freshly ground pepper

4 racks of lamb, trimmed of excess fat

Ionian Garlic Sauce (recipe follows)

1. Combine 1¼ cups of the olive oil with the lemon juice, garlic, oregano, savory, and salt and pepper to taste in a small mixing bowl.

2. Place the lamb in a glass baking dish and pour the marinade over the lamb, turning to coat all sides. Then lay each rack meat side down, cover the dish with plastic wrap, and refrigerate for 12 hours.

3. Preheat and oil the grill. Remove the lamb from the refrigerator. Using your fingertips, remove excess marinade from the racks, allowing the mixture to drip back into the dish.

4. Season the racks with salt and pepper to taste and place them, meat side down, on the hot grill. Grill for 3 minutes and then turn and grill the remaining side for 3 minutes. Transfer to a platter and let rest for a few minutes. The lamb will still be cold and raw in the center.

5. Cut the lamb racks into individual chops. (You may save the end chops, which are sometimes not as nice as the center, for a salad or snack.) Using a pastry brush, lightly coat each chop with some of the remaining ¼ cup olive oil. Season with salt and pepper to taste.

6. Return the grill to medium-high heat. When hot, add the chops, in batches of 4 to 5, and grill for about 2 minutes, or just long enough to mark the meat with the grill. Turn slightly and grill for another 2 minutes, or just long enough to burn a crosshatch into the meat. Continue to grill for another 2 minutes

Botsacos on Lamb
Greek lamb is tiny; I try to mimic its size and flavor by marinating whole racks, searing them on the grill, then cutting them into chops to finish grilling. The result is a thin chop with an extra layer of charred flavor. To save time, you can just grill baby lamb chops (18 to 24 for this recipe, depending on their size).

Editor's Note

This herbaceous sauce is not only great with lamb dishes, it can also be warmed and served over pan-roasted fish fillets, which benefit from the brightness of the vinegar and lemon.

for rare, or until the chops are nicely browned and cooked to your desired degree of doneness. Arrange the grilled chops on a serving platter and serve with Ionian Garlic Sauce on the side.

Ionian Garlic Sauce

MAKES ABOUT 1½ CUPS

½ cup roughly chopped fresh flat-leaf parsley leaves

½ cup roughly chopped fresh dill

½ cup roughly chopped fresh mint

½ cup roughly chopped watercress leaves

¼ cup roughly chopped fresh oregano leaves

About 1 teaspoon coarse salt

1 lemon

2 garlic cloves, peeled

¼ cup red wine vinegar

1½ tablespoons sugar

About ½ cup extra virgin olive oil

1. Place the parsley, dill, mint, watercress, and oregano on a cutting board. Evenly sprinkle the salt over the mixture. The salt will cause the herbs and watercress to begin to "weep" their liquid.

2. Pull the herbs and watercress together in the center of the board and sprinkle with the juice of ½ lemon. Using a sharp knife, begin chopping the herbs and watercress until a very fine, moist mixture has formed. Set aside.

3. Place the garlic on a clean cutting board along with a pinch of salt and, using a sharp knife, work the garlic into a paste.

4. Combine the juice of the remaining lemon half with the vinegar and sugar in a small mixing bowl. Add the reserved herbs and garlic and season with salt to taste. Add just enough olive oil to make a vinaigrette. Reserve, covered, at room temperature until ready to use.

best of the best exclusive

Sautéed Sweet Peppers with Toasted Garlic and Capers

6 SERVINGS

5   tablespoons extra-virgin olive oil
2   large red bell peppers, sliced lengthwise ½ inch thick
2   large yellow bell peppers, sliced lengthwise ½ inch thick
Kosher salt
8   large garlic cloves, thinly sliced
1   tablespoon capers, drained

1. In a large, deep skillet, heat 3 tablespoons of the olive oil. Add the peppers and season with salt. Cover and cook over moderate heat, stirring occasionally, until softened, about 18 minutes. Transfer the peppers and their juices to a bowl.

2. Wipe out the skillet. Heat the remaining 2 tablespoons of olive oil in the skillet. Add the garlic and cook over moderate heat until golden, about 3 minutes. Add the capers and the reserved peppers and their juices. Cook, tossing, until the peppers are warm; season with salt. Transfer the peppers to a bowl and serve warm or at room temperature.

MAKE AHEAD The peppers can be refrigerated for up to 5 days.

Editor's Note

Whenever Botsacos makes a pot of his meat-filled Sunday spaghetti sauce, he also cooks up these sweet, juicy peppers so he can drape strips of them on top of the pasta. These peppers are equally delicious tossed with plain pasta, tucked into sandwiches or served with roasted or grilled meats.

Duck with Green
Picholine Olives, p. 24

Braise

By Daniel Boulud & Melissa Clark

To create the definitive book on braises, star chef Daniel Boulud assembled an international roster of his favorites, from simple (Spicy Merguez with Spinach and White Beans) to more complex (Beef Short Ribs with Daikon Radish and Shiitake). All the recipes involve a long, slow oven-braise, and this work-free period is the technique's real advantage. "I always joke that braising is a good technique for newlyweds," Boulud teases. "It gives them plenty of time to pursue other things while their dinner cooks."

Published by Ecco, $32.50.
Find more recipes by Daniel Boulud at foodandwine.com/boulud

Duck with Green Picholine Olives

Editor's Note

If you love crispy skin, take the braised duck legs out of the sauce and place them, skin side up, on a baking pan. Broil, watching carefully, until the skin is browned and crisp. Serve the duck with the sauce.

Cooking duck with olives has been a classic method ever since olives became fashionable in France about 100 years ago. Their brininess and acidity work well with the richness of the duck meat. Serve this with crusty bread, because there will be plenty of good sauce for mopping up.

MAKES 4 SERVINGS

4 to 6 duck legs (about 3 pounds)
Coarse sea salt or kosher salt and freshly ground black pepper
   2 tablespoons extra-virgin olive oil
   ¼ pound sliced bacon, cut into ¼-inch pieces
   3 carrots, peeled, trimmed, and diced
   2 small onions, peeled and chopped
   2 small turnips, peeled and diced
   ½ cup green picholine olives, pitted
   2 sprigs fresh thyme
   1 bay leaf
   2 cups chicken stock (recipe follows) or low-sodium canned broth

1. The night before you plan to serve this dish, place a rack in the lower third of the oven and preheat the oven to 350°F.

2. Season the duck with salt and pepper. Heat the olive oil in a medium cast-iron pot or Dutch oven over medium-high heat. Add the duck legs and sear until golden brown on all sides, 7 to 10 minutes.

3. Transfer the duck to a platter. Pour off the excess fat from the pot. Return the duck to the pot along with the bacon and cook, stirring, over medium-high heat for 5 to 6 minutes. Spoon any fat out of the pot. Add the carrots, onions, turnips, olives, thyme, and bay leaf, and stock. Transfer the pot to the oven and braise, covered, for 2 hours, until the duck is tender. Chill overnight.

4. Preheat the oven to 350°F. Remove the layer of fat from the top of the sauce and heat the duck in the oven for 30 minutes. Remove the thyme sprigs and bay leaf and serve.

Chicken Stock

MAKES ABOUT 1 GALLON

- 4 pounds chicken necks, backs, and wings or chicken parts, skinned, fat trimmed, and rinsed
- 2 medium onions, peeled and quartered
- 2 small carrots, peeled and cut into 2-inch pieces
- 1 stalk celery, trimmed and cut into 2-inch pieces
- 1 medium leek, trimmed, split lengthwise, and washed
- 1 head garlic, split in half crosswise
- 1 bay leaf
- 5 sprigs fresh flat-leaf parsley
- 1 teaspoon white peppercorns

1. Put the chicken and 7 quarts cold water in a tall stockpot and bring to a boil. Add 3 quarts more cold water (it should be very cold) and bring to a boil; skim off any fat that rises to the top. Lower the heat so that the water simmers, and simmer—skimming regularly—for 10 minutes.

2. Add the remaining ingredients to the pot and simmer for 3 hours, continuing to skim so that the stock will be clear. Strain the stock through a colander. Allow the solids to drain for a few minutes before discarding them, then strain the stock through a chinois or fine-mesh sieve. Let cool to room temperature, then cover tightly and refrigerate. (The stock can be kept tightly covered in the refrigerator for up to 4 days or frozen for up to 1 month.)

Beef Short Ribs with Daikon Radish and Shiitake

I grew up eating pot-au-feu (poached beef and vegetables) made with short ribs, so when I think of short ribs, I always imagine them poached, carved, and served off the bone in nice slices, maybe topped with a little broth and some coarse salt. But short ribs are also one of the most fantastic cuts for braising. They are meaty and full of gelatin and fat. When you have cooked them slowly, they will start to melt almost before you even get a bite into your mouth. Since you cook them on the bone, they have a lot of flavor, which the browning in a braise recipe will intensify, giving them a very earthy, caramelized, full taste. You can season braised short ribs any way you want, even strongly—as I do here, with a combination of dark soy sauce, ginger, star anise, and Szechuan pepper. They can take it!

When you are buying short ribs, tell the butcher you want them cut thick and lean (leanness is relative; even the leanest part of the short rib is pretty fatty). The pieces should be about 2 to 3 inches wide, weighing 1 pound each. Sometimes the butcher may precut the meat into smaller, thinner pieces. These will work too, but you might end up with more fat, which will dissolve into the sauce. Just skim it off with a spoon after cooking. If you have time, cook this the day before serving; let it cool, and refrigerate it overnight. That makes it very easy to take the fat off before you reheat the ribs.

MAKES 4 TO 6 SERVINGS

- 3 tablespoons extra-virgin olive oil
- 3 pounds short ribs, trimmed of excess fat

Coarse sea salt or kosher salt and freshly ground black pepper

- 2 large red onions, peeled and cut into 1-inch cubes
- 1 (2-inch) piece fresh gingerroot, peeled and finely grated
- ½ pound shiitake mushrooms, cut into ½-inch-thick slices
- 2 star anise pods
- 1½ teaspoons ground Szechuan peppercorns
- ½ teaspoon ground cardamom
- 2 cups beef stock (recipe follows) or low-sodium canned beef broth

2 tablespoons fermented hot black bean paste

1 tablespoon dark soy sauce

2 pounds daikon radish, peeled, trimmed, and cut into ½-inch-thick slices

1 bunch scallions, trimmed and sliced

1 garlic clove, peeled and finely chopped

6 sprigs fresh cilantro, leaves only

Cucumber-Radish Rémoulade, for serving (page 29)

1. Center a rack in the oven and preheat the oven to 275°F.

2. In a medium cast-iron pot or Dutch oven over high heat, warm 2 tablespoons of the olive oil. Season the short ribs with salt and pepper and sear until golden brown on all sides, 15 to 20 minutes. Remove the short ribs and pour off all but 2 tablespoons of the fat from the pot.

3. Add the onions, gingerroot, and mushrooms and sauté, stirring, until the vegetables are softened, 5 to 6 minutes. Add the star anise, Szechuan pepper, and cardamom and cook, stirring, for 1 minute. Stir in the beef stock, bean paste, and soy sauce. Add the daikon radish and return the short ribs to the pot. Bring to a simmer.

4. Cover the pot and transfer it to the oven. Braise for 4 hours, or until the meat is very tender, checking the short ribs occasionally and spooning off any excess fat that rises to the surface. If the sauce is too thin or is not flavored intensely enough, ladle most of it off into another pot and simmer it until it thickens and intensifies. Then add it back to the first pot.

5. To serve: In a medium skillet over medium heat, warm the remaining 1 tablespoon olive oil. Add the scallions and garlic and cook until softened, 1 to 2 minutes. Sprinkle the scallion mixture and cilantro leaves over the short ribs. Serve with Cucumber-Radish Rémoulade.

Braise
By Daniel Boulud
& Melissa Clark

Editor's Note

Black bean paste is made from soybeans that have been salted and fermented. Many different varieties of bean paste are available (some with chiles, others with garlic) at supermarkets and Asian markets; Boulud says any will work with this recipe.

Beef Stock

MAKES ABOUT 5 QUARTS

1 large onion, peeled, and halved crosswise

2 whole cloves

1 (6-pound) bone-in beef shank, cut crosswise into 2-inch-thick slices and trimmed of excess fat (ask your butcher to do this for you)

Coarse sea salt or kosher salt and freshly ground black pepper

2 tablespoons vegetable oil

6 large white mushrooms, trimmed, cleaned, and halved

4 stalks celery, trimmed and cut into 2-inch pieces

3 carrots, peeled, trimmed, and cut into 1-inch pieces

6 garlic cloves, peeled and crushed

5 sprigs fresh flat-leaf parsley

2 sprigs fresh thyme

2 bay leaves

1 teaspoon coriander seeds, toasted

1. Heat a griddle or small cast-iron skillet over high heat. Place the onion halves in the pan, cut side down, and cook until blackened (they should be as dark as you can get them). Transfer the onion to a plate and stick 1 whole clove in each half.

2. Season the beef with salt and pepper. Heat the oil in a large nonstick skillet over high heat. Working in batches, sear the beef until well browned on all sides, about 20 minutes per batch. As the pieces of meat are browned, transfer them to a large stockpot.

3. When all the meat is browned and in the stockpot, pour in 6 quarts water, add the remaining ingredients, and bring the liquid to a boil. Lower the heat to a simmer and cook for 2 hours, frequently skimming off the foam and fat that bubble to the surface.

4. Strain the stock through a colander and then pass it through a chinois or fine-mesh sieve. Let cool to room temperature, then cover and refrigerate. (The stock can be kept tightly covered in the refrigerator for up to 4 days or in the freezer for up to 1 month.) When the stock is chilled, the fat will rise to the top. Before reheating the stock, spoon off and discard the fat.

Cucumber-Radish Rémoulade

MAKES 4 TO 6 SERVINGS

- 2 tablespoons mayonnaise
- 1 tablespoon Dijon mustard
- 2 teaspoons wasabi paste

Coarse sea salt or kosher salt and freshly ground black pepper

- 1 pound hothouse cucumbers, peeled, seeded, and cut into 1½-by-¼-inch sticks
- ½ pound red radishes, trimmed and cut into ⅛-inch-thick slices
- 3 tablespoons finely minced fresh chives

1. In a small mixing bowl, combine the mayonnaise, mustard, and wasabi paste. Season to taste with salt and pepper.

2. In a large mixing bowl, combine the cucumbers, radishes, and chives. Gently fold in the mayonnaise mixture and season with more salt and pepper. Serve immediately.

Spicy Merguez with Spinach and White Beans

Merguez is a very spicy North African sausage usually made from lamb or a combination of lamb and beef. People in France, especially Paris, love these sausages and eat them grilled and stuffed into a baguette, with pommes frites and maybe some harissa (hot sauce) spooned on top. This combination is called merguez frites, and we French eat it on the streets the way Americans eat hot dogs. Delicious!

You can buy merguez at butcher shops and large supermarkets, in links or rolled into a coil. The coil makes a very nice presentation. Just secure it with toothpicks before searing and braising, then remember to take them out before serving.

MAKES 4 TO 6 SERVINGS

- ¼ cup plus 1 tablespoon extra-virgin olive oil
- 4 pounds spinach, stems removed, washed and dried
- 2 medium onions, peeled and cut into small cubes
- 6 garlic cloves, peeled and finely chopped
- 2 tablespoons chopped fresh mint leaves
- 2 tablespoons chopped fresh cilantro leaves
- 1 tablespoon harissa (see Harissa, page 32) or ¼ teaspoon cayenne pepper
- 1 teaspoon freshly ground black pepper
- ½ teaspoon Four-Spice Powder (recipe follows)
- ½ pound dried cannellini beans or black-eyed peas, soaked overnight in cold water and drained
- 2 pounds merguez sausage: 1 long link or individual links
- ¼ cup freshly squeezed lemon juice (about 2 lemons)

Coarse sea salt or kosher salt

1. Center a rack in the oven and preheat the oven to 300°F.

2. Heat ¼ cup of the olive oil in a wide cast-iron pot or Dutch oven over high heat. Add the spinach, little by little, and cook, stirring continuously, until all the spinach has wilted and browned slightly and all the liquid has evaporated, 20 to 30 minutes.

3. Add the onions, garlic, mint, cilantro, harissa (or cayenne), black pepper, and Four-Spice Powder and cook, stirring, for 5 minutes.

4. Pour in 4 cups water and add the cannellini beans (or black-eyed peas). Stir, bring to a simmer, and cover. Braise in the oven for 2 hours, or until the beans are nearly tender.

5. Meanwhile, heat the remaining 1 tablespoon olive oil in a medium skillet over medium heat. Sear the merguez on all sides, about 10 minutes. Transfer to a plate lined with a paper towel to drain.

6. Stir the lemon juice into the beans and place the seared merguez on top. Cover and continue to braise until the beans are tender and the sausage is cooked through, about 30 minutes more. Season with salt to taste.

HARISSA Both a condiment and a seasoning for soups and tagines, harissa is an essential ingredient in North African cooking, particularly in Tunisia, Algeria, and Morocco. It gets its hot, smoky essence from a mix of dried chile peppers, cumin, coriander, garlic, caraway, olive oil, and occasionally tomatoes. The sauce is such an important part of Tunisian cooking that connoisseurs claim to be able to distinguish between the flavor of chiles that have been dried in the sun, the shade, or an oven. It can be purchased at specialty supermarkets or online.

Four-Spice Powder

Used by the French to season hearty, rustic food like charcuterie, stews, and braised game, four-spice powder is traditionally a blend of cloves, pepper, nutmeg, and ginger. It is also used in the French-influenced cuisine of North Africa, where it fits in nicely with the tagines and stews of that region. This recipe makes only a small batch, but if you think you'll be using a lot of four-spice, you can double or triple it and store it in an airtight container in a cool, dry place for up to 6 months. Four-spice blends can also be purchased at specialty spice markets and online.

MAKES ABOUT 2 TABLESPOONS

- 2 teaspoons whole cloves
- 1 heaping tablespoon black peppercorns
- 2 teaspoons freshly grated nutmeg
- 1 teaspoon ground ginger

In a spice grinder or clean coffee grinder, finely grind the cloves and black pepper together. Transfer to a bowl and combine with the nutmeg and ginger.

Editor's Note

To save time, don't prepare this recipe for the merguez dish. Instead, just add a small pinch each of ground cloves, black pepper and ginger to the pot, and grate in a little nutmeg.

Lemon-Coriander Basmati Pilaf

MAKES 6 SERVINGS

  1 lemon
  2 tablespoons unsalted butter
  1 small onion, peeled and finely chopped
  2 cups basmati rice, rinsed
½ teaspoon crushed coriander seeds
  1 cup milk
  2 teaspoons coarse sea salt or kosher salt

Finely grate the zest of one half of the lemon and juice the entire lemon. In a medium saucepan over medium heat, melt the butter. Add the onion and cook, stirring occasionally, until tender, 3 to 5 minutes. Add the rice and sauté for 3 minutes. Stir in the lemon zest and juice and the coriander seeds. Add 3 cups water and bring to a boil. Add the milk and salt and return to a boil. Reduce the heat to low, cover, and simmer for 15 minutes. Remove from the heat and let sit, covered, for 5 minutes before serving.

best of the best exclusive
Crab Salad

4 SERVINGS

- ¼ cup walnuts
- 1 tablespoon mayonnaise
- 2 tablespoons extra-virgin olive oil
- 4 teaspoons fresh lemon juice
- 1 small celery rib, cut into ⅛-inch dice
- 2 tablespoons finely diced celery root
- 2 tablespoons finely diced Granny Smith apple
- 1½ teaspoons finely chopped tarragon
- 1 pound lump crabmeat, picked over

Kosher salt and freshly ground pepper

- 1 head of frisée, coarsely chopped

1. Preheat the oven to 350°. Spread the walnuts in a pie plate and toast for 8 minutes, until fragrant. Transfer to a plate and let cool. Coarsely chop the walnuts.

2. In a medium bowl, mix the mayonnaise with 1 tablespoon of the olive oil and 2 teaspoons of the lemon juice. Stir in the celery, celery root, apple and tarragon. Gently fold in the crabmeat and walnuts and season with salt and pepper.

3. In a medium bowl, mix the remaining 1 tablespoon of olive oil and 2 teaspoons of lemon juice. Add the frisée and toss. Season the salad with salt and pepper. Transfer the frisée to plates, top with the crab salad and serve.

MAKE AHEAD The crab salad can be refrigerated for up to 4 hours; fold in the walnuts just before serving.

Editor's Note

A cross between a seafood and Waldorf salad, this elegant recipe is a streamlined version of a dish on the menu at Boulud's restaurant Daniel in New York City, where it is served with apple gelée and celery root remoulade.

Individual Meringue Cups with
Lime Cream and Fresh Berries, p. 38

The Cake Book

By Tish Boyle

As editor of *Chocolatier* and *Pastry Art & Design* magazines, Tish Boyle has learned more than a few tricks of the trade when it comes to desserts. In her eighth cookbook, she shares many of them in nearly 200 recipes that are rated by difficulty, making it an excellent reference for both novice and experienced bakers. Included are useful decorating tips, a great section on troubleshooting (if a cake turns out dry, brush it with simple syrup and frost generously), and just plain delicious recipes like Creamy Pumpkin Cheesecake with Ginger-Pecan Crust.

Published by John Wiley & Sons, Inc., $39.95.

Individual Meringue Cups with Lime Cream and Fresh Berries

Boyle on Meringue

Meringue is versatile. If you end up with leftovers after forming the shells, pipe it in little dollops on a cookie sheet and bake until crisp. You can dip the bottoms of the meringues in melted chocolate, sandwich them together with ganache or crumble them over ice cream.

With its crown of glistening sugared berries, tart lime filling, and crunchy meringue base, this dessert looks like it could have come straight from a toney Paris pâtisserie. The meringue shells can be made up to five days ahead and then filled and garnished a few hours before serving.

MAKES 6 INDIVIDUAL MERINGUES

MERINGUE CUPS

4 large egg whites, at room temperature

Pinch of salt

¼ teaspoon cream of tartar

1 cup (7 ounces/200 grams) superfine sugar

LIME CREAM AND FRUIT TOPPING

4 large egg yolks

½ cup (3.5 ounces/100 grams) granulated sugar

6 tablespoons freshly squeezed lime juice

4 tablespoons (2 ounces/57 grams) unsalted butter, cut into tablespoons

1 teaspoon finely grated lime zest

¾ cup heavy cream

2 cups (8 ounces/227 grams) mixed fresh raspberries, sliced strawberries, and red currants

Confectioners' sugar for dusting

MAKE THE MERINGUES

1. Position a rack in the center of the oven and preheat the oven to 225°F. Trace six 3½-inch circles onto a sheet of parchment paper. Turn the parchment paper upside down and place it on the baking sheet.

2. In the bowl of an electric mixer, using the whisk attachment, beat the egg whites at medium speed until foamy. Add the salt and cream of tartar and beat at medium-high speed until soft peaks begin to form. Gradually add the sugar, about 1 tablespoon at a time, then increase the speed to high and beat the whites until stiff peaks form.

3. Scrape the meringue into a large (18-inch) pastry bag fitted with a medium plain tip (such as Ateco #4). Starting in the center of each circle, pipe a spiral of meringue in toward the edge, filling the circle completely. Pipe a ring of meringue around the edge of each circle. Pipe another ring of meringue on top of the first, to form cups.

4. Bake the meringues for 2 hours, or until they are very lightly colored and dry to the touch. Let them cool completely.

MAKE THE LIME CREAM

5. Set a fine-mesh sieve over a medium bowl and set aside. In a medium heavy nonreactive saucepan, whisk the egg yolks and sugar until blended. Stir in the lime juice and butter, and cook over medium heat, whisking constantly, until the mixture turns opaque and thickens enough to leave a path on the back of a wooden spoon when you draw your finger across it. Remove the pan from the heat and immediately strain the custard through the sieve, pressing it through with a rubber spatula. Stir in the lime zest. Set the mixture aside while you whip the cream. Or refrigerate the mixture, covered, until ready to use.

6. Shortly before serving, in the bowl of an electric mixer, using the whisk attachment, beat the heavy cream at high speed until medium-firm peaks form. Place the bowl of whipped cream in the refrigerator.

7. If the lime mixture has not been refrigerated, set the bowl containing the lime mixture in a large bowl filled about one-third of the way with ice water (be careful that the water doesn't splash into the lime mixture). Stir the mixture frequently until it is slightly cooler than room temperature, about 10 minutes.

8. Fold a large spoonful of the whipped cream into the lime base to lighten it. Gently fold in the remaining cream.

9. Spoon the lime cream into the meringue cups. Top each meringue with mixed berries, then dust lightly with confectioners' sugar and serve.

Rich Marble Pound Cake with Chocolate Glaze

This very tender cake features a stunning striated pattern of alternating vanilla and deep chocolate batter. It is a big, over-the-top pound cake made all the more elegant with a coating of shiny dark chocolate glaze. If you prefer a more homespun version, skip the glaze and dust with confectioners' sugar.

MAKES ONE 10-INCH BUNDT CAKE, SERVING 12 TO 14

- 3 cups (12 ounces/342 grams) cake flour
- 2 teaspoons baking powder
- ½ teaspoon salt
- 2½ cups (17.6 ounces/500 grams) granulated sugar, divided
- ½ cup (1.4 ounces/41 grams) natural (not Dutch-processed) cocoa powder
- 6 tablespoons water
- 1½ cups (3 sticks/12 ounces/340 grams) unsalted butter, softened
- 1½ teaspoons vanilla extract
- 5 large eggs
- ½ cup whole milk
- ⅔ cup Bittersweet Chocolate Glaze (recipe follows)

MAKE THE CAKE

1. Position a rack in the center of the oven and preheat the oven to 325°F. Grease the inside of a 10-inch Bundt pan. Dust the pan with flour.

2. Sift together the flour, baking powder, and salt into a medium bowl. Set aside.

3. In a medium bowl, whisk together ½ cup of the sugar, the cocoa powder, and water until smooth; set aside.

4. In the bowl of an electric mixer, using the paddle attachment, beat the butter at medium speed until very creamy, about 2 minutes. Gradually beat in the remaining 2 cups sugar. Increase the speed to medium-high and beat until the mixture is well blended and light, about 4 minutes. At medium speed, beat in the vanilla, then beat in the eggs one at a time, mixing well after each addition and scraping down the sides of the bowl as necessary.

Boyle on Flour

Cake flour creates a slightly more tender crumb than all-purpose flour. If you want to substitute all-purpose in a recipe that calls for cake flour, reduce the flour by 2 tablespoons per cup and replace it with 2 tablespoons of cornstarch.

**Boyle on
Glazed Cakes**
This glossy dark
chocolate glaze will
enhance a variety
of cakes. When chilled,
it becomes dull and
slightly hard, so be sure
to bring the cake back
to room temperature
before serving it.

At low speed, add the dry ingredients in three additions, alternating with the milk in two additions and mixing just until blended.

5. Add 3 cups of the batter to the cocoa mixture and stir until blended. Spoon one-third of the remaining plain batter into the prepared pan and smooth it into an even layer. Spoon one-third of the chocolate batter over the plain batter and smooth it into an even layer. Spoon over another third of the plain batter, then another third of the chocolate batter, smoothing the layers. Repeat with the remaining batters, ending with the chocolate batter.

6. Bake the cake for 60 to 70 minutes, until a cake tester inserted into the center comes out clean. Cool the cake in the pan on a wire rack for 15 minutes.

7. Invert the cake onto the rack and cool completely.

GLAZE THE CAKE

8. Place the cake on the rack, on a wax paper– or foil-lined baking sheet. Slowly pour the glaze over the top of the cake, letting it drip down the sides of the cake. Let the glaze set for about 30 minutes before slicing the cake.

Bittersweet Chocolate Glaze

TO DRIZZLE ONTO THE TOP OF A 9- OR 10-INCH CAKE (MAKES ⅔ CUP)

   3 ounces (85 grams) bittersweet chocolate, coarsely chopped
 ⅓ cup heavy cream
 ½ teaspoon vanilla extract

1. Place the chocolate in the bowl of a food processor and process just until finely ground. (Leave the chocolate in the processor.)

2. In a small saucepan, bring the cream to a boil. Remove from the heat and add the chocolate to the pan. Stir until the chocolate is completely melted and the glaze is smooth. Stir in the vanilla extract. Transfer the glaze to a small bowl. Cover the surface of the glaze with a piece of plastic wrap and let cool for about 10 minutes before using.

Creamy Pumpkin Cheesecake with Ginger-Pecan Crust

MAKES ONE 9-INCH CAKE, SERVING 12 TO 16

GINGER-PECAN CRUST

- 1 cup (4.3 ounces/121 grams) all-purpose flour
- ¼ cup (1.9 ounces/54 grams) firmly packed light brown sugar
- ⅛ teaspoon salt
- ⅓ cup (1.2 ounces/33 grams) pecans
- ¼ cup (1.4 ounces/40 grams) chopped crystallized ginger
- ½ cup (1 stick/4 ounces/113 grams) cold unsalted butter, cut into ½-inch cubes
- 1 tablespoon cold water

PUMPKIN CHEESECAKE FILLING

- 1 cup pumpkin puree
- ½ cup heavy cream
- 2 teaspoons vanilla extract
- 1 teaspoon ground cinnamon
- ½ teaspoon ground ginger
- ¼ teaspoon freshly grated nutmeg
- ¼ teaspoon salt
- 1¼ pounds (567 grams) cream cheese, softened
- ½ cup (3.5 ounces/100 grams) granulated sugar
- ½ cup (3.8 ounces/108 grams) firmly packed light brown sugar
- 1 tablespoon (0.3 ounces/7 grams) cornstarch
- 4 large eggs

SUGARED PUMPKIN SEEDS

- ½ cup (2.5 ounces/70 grams) hulled raw pumpkin seeds
- 1 large egg white

Pinch of salt

- 2 tablespoons (0.9 ounces/25 grams) granulated sugar
- ⅛ teaspoon ground cinnamon

Creamy Pumpkin Cheesecake
with Ginger-Pecan Crust

GARNISH

Classic Whipped Cream (recipe follows)

MAKE THE CRUST

1. Position a rack in the center of the oven and preheat the oven to 350°F. Lightly grease the bottom and sides of a 9 x 3-inch springform pan. Cut an 18-inch square of heavy-duty aluminum foil and wrap the foil around the outside of the pan.

2. Place the flour, sugar, salt, pecans, and ginger in the bowl of a food processor and process until the pecans are finely ground. Add the butter and process until the mixture forms coarse crumbs. Add the water and process until the dough starts to come together. Press the dough into an even layer over the bottom of the prepared pan.

3. Bake the crust for 25 to 30 minutes, until it is just beginning to brown. Place the pan on a wire rack and cool completely. Reduce the oven temperature to 325°F.

MAKE THE FILLING

4. In a medium bowl, whisk together the pumpkin puree, heavy cream, vanilla extract, cinnamon, ginger, nutmeg, and salt. Set aside.

5. In the bowl of an electric mixer, using the paddle attachment, beat the cream cheese at medium-low speed until creamy, about 2 minutes, scraping down the sides of the bowl as necessary. Gradually add the sugars and beat until blended. Add the pumpkin mixture and mix until blended. Add the cornstarch and mix just until combined. Add the eggs one at a time, mixing well after each addition and scraping down the sides of the bowl as necessary.

6. Scrape the batter into the cooled crust. Place the wrapped pan in a roasting pan or large baking pan. Pour enough hot water into the roasting pan to come 1 inch up the sides of the springform pan. Bake the cheesecake in the water bath for 70 to 80 minutes, until the center of the cake is set but slightly wobbly (the cake will set completely as it cools).

Boyle on Sugared Seeds and Nuts

Sugaring pumpkin seeds after tossing them with egg white is an old French technique that is not used much in this country. It's easy and also works well with nuts—try it on pecans. Sugared nuts make a wonderful garnish or snack.

7. Remove the cake pan from the water bath, place the pan on a wire rack, and carefully loosen the foil. Immediately run the tip of a paring knife around the sides of the pan, to prevent the top from cracking. Let the cake cool completely.

8. Refrigerate the cheesecake for at least 4 hours before serving.

MAKE THE PUMPKIN SEEDS

9. Position a rack in the center of the oven and preheat the oven to 325°F. Lightly grease a baking sheet.

10. Place the pumpkin seeds in a small bowl. In another small bowl, whisk the egg white just until frothy. Add just enough of the egg white to the pumpkin seeds to coat them. Add the salt, sugar, and cinnamon, and toss well to coat the seeds.

11. Spread the seeds in a single layer on the prepared baking sheet. Bake, tossing them occasionally with a metal spatula, for 15 to 20 minutes, until they begin to dry and color. Place the pan on a wire rack and cool completely.

12. With your fingers, separate any clumps of seeds. (The seeds can be stored in an airtight container for up to a week.)

13. To serve, remove the side of the pan and slice the cake with a thin-bladed sharp knife, wiping the knife clean between each cut. Garnish each slice with a dollop of whipped cream and a sprinkling of sugared pumpkin seeds.

STORE in the refrigerator, loosely covered, for up to 5 days.

Classic Whipped Cream

A dollop of freshly whipped cream improves almost any cake, from a simple
pound cake to an intensely flavored flourless chocolate cake, and takes
minutes to make.

MAKES 3 CUPS

1½ cups heavy cream

  3 tablespoons (0.7 ounces/21 grams) confectioners' sugar, sifted

1½ teaspoons vanilla extract

In the chilled bowl of an electric mixer, using the whisk attachment,
whip the cream at high speed just until it begins to thicken. Add the sugar
and vanilla and beat until soft peaks form. Use immediately, or cover
and refrigerate.

STORE in the refrigerator, covered, for up to 2 hours.

best of the best exclusive

Lemon Tart in a Pistachio Crust

Editor's Note

Pistachios lend this tart crust a speckled look, a soft, cookie-like texture and a mild, nutty flavor. They are a wonderful complement to the tangy lemon filling.

MAKES ONE 11-INCH TART

PASTRY AND GARNISH

½ cup plus ⅓ cup shelled, unsalted pistachios (4 ounces)

¾ cup confectioners' sugar

1½ cups all-purpose flour, plus more for dusting

⅛ teaspoon salt

1 stick cold unsalted butter, cut into ½-inch dice

1 large egg, lightly beaten

1 large egg white, lightly beaten

FILLING

3 large egg yolks

2 large eggs

1 cup granulated sugar

⅔ cup fresh lemon juice

7 tablespoons cold unsalted butter, cut into 1-inch dice

Lightly sweetened whipped cream, for serving

1. MAKE THE PASTRY: Preheat the oven to 350°F. Spread the pistachios on a rimmed baking sheet and toast for about 7 minutes, until fragrant; let cool completely. Coarsely chop ⅓ cup of the pistachios and reserve for garnish.

2. In a food processor, process the remaining ½ cup of whole pistachios with the confectioners' sugar until the nuts are very finely ground, about 1 minute. Add the 1½ cups of flour and the salt and pulse to blend. Add the butter and pulse just until it is the size of peas. Add the whole egg and pulse just until the pastry is evenly moistened. Turn the pastry out onto a lightly floured work surface and gather it into a ball. Flatten the pastry into a disk, wrap it in plastic and refrigerate for 1 hour, or until firm.

3. On a lightly floured surface, roll out the pastry to a 15-inch round. Transfer the pastry to an 11-inch round fluted tart pan with a removable bottom. Trim the overhang and use the trimmings to patch any cracks. Prick the bottom of the tart shell all over with a fork and refrigerate until chilled, about 30 minutes.

4. Line the tart shell with foil and fill with pie weights or dried beans. Bake for 20 minutes, or until the pastry is set. Remove the pie weights and foil and bake for 15 minutes longer, until the pastry is light golden and just cooked through. Immediately brush the tart shell with the beaten egg white to fill any holes or cracks. Transfer to a rack to cool.

5. MAKE THE FILLING: In a medium heatproof bowl, whisk the egg yolks and whole eggs with the sugar and lemon juice. Set the bowl over (but not in) a pan of simmering water and cook, whisking constantly, until the mixture is thick, about 8 minutes. Remove the bowl from the heat and whisk in the butter, a few pieces at a time, until fully incorporated. Pour the filling into the tart shell and bake for 18 minutes, or until the center is just set. Transfer the tart to a rack to cool completely, about 2 hours.

6. To serve, cut the tart into wedges. Top each wedge with a dollop of whipped cream and sprinkle with the reserved chopped pistachios.

MAKE AHEAD The baked tart can be refrigerated overnight.

Some ingredients for Duck Breasts with
Radishes, Anchovy, and Orange, p. 52

The Red Cat Cookbook

By Jimmy Bradley & Andrew Friedman

Since chef Jimmy Bradley opened The Red Cat restaurant in Manhattan in 1999, his menu has been an inspired mix of Italian-American and New England–style dishes, a reflection of his own background. His simple, hearty recipes, Bradley says, are very different from the kind most chefs prefer: "Many chefs are interested in the grandiose, and I'm really more interested in using five ingredients or less." A prime example is his clever Quick Sauté of Zucchini, made with only zucchini, olive oil, almonds and pecorino cheese.

Published by Clarkson Potter, $35.
Find more recipes by Jimmy Bradley at foodandwine.com/bradley

Duck Breasts with Radishes, Anchovy, and Orange

Laurence Edelman, The Red Cat's sous-chef, made this for me one day. When he told me the ingredients, I thought I must have misunderstood him: duck, radishes, anchovy, and orange. What was he thinking? But once I tasted it I found it to be such a unique, wonderful, and totally unexpected combination of ingredients that I knew I wanted to put it in the book. The seemingly disparate flavors all play smartly off the duck and each other— the salty anchovy against the peppery radish, with the bright orange and herbaceous parsley livening the whole affair.

SERVES 4

4 Pekin (Long Island) duck breasts, 6 to 8 ounces each

Salt

Freshly ground black pepper

2 tablespoons butter

12 French breakfast radishes, quartered or halved lengthwise, depending on size

8 anchovy fillets, mashed to a paste with 1 teaspoon Dijon mustard

1 tablespoon lemon juice

¼ cup sliced parsley

1 orange, separated into segments (see grapefruit instructions, page 56)

½ cup celery leaves

Extra-virgin olive oil, for drizzling

Preheat the oven to 350°F.

Heat a large, ovenproof skillet, preferably cast-iron, over medium heat. Score the duck skin a few times with a very sharp knife, and season the duck breasts with salt and pepper. Add the breasts to the pan, skin side down, and cook until the fat has rendered from the skin and the skin has turned nicely brown and crispy, approximately 15 minutes. Drain the fat from the pan and discard. Transfer to the oven and cook for approximately 7 minutes for medium rare, or longer for more well done.

When the duck breasts are done, transfer them to a cutting board and let rest for 5 minutes.

While the duck is cooking, melt the butter in a heavy-bottomed sauté pan. Add the radishes and sauté until lightly browned, approximately 4 minutes. Add the anchovy paste and mix well with a spoon to coat the radishes with the paste. Season with salt and pepper. Add the lemon juice and parsley, taste, and adjust the seasoning with salt and pepper.

Slice the duck breasts into thin slices. Spoon some radishes onto each of 4 dinner plates. Arrange the slices of 1 duck breast around the radishes on each plate. Garnish with the orange segments and celery leaves. Drizzle with olive oil and sprinkle with salt. Serve.

Quick Sauté of Zucchini with Toasted Almonds and Pecorino

We've served this dish at The Red Cat since our first dinner back in 1999. It sums up a lot of what I think makes a dish comfortable to both cook and diner: a mere handful of ingredients, each contributing its own important flavor and texture; the whole thing held together with a fine extra-virgin olive oil. It's that simple, but the flavor is very complex and complete.

Technically speaking, "quick sauté" is almost redundant; to sauté something means to make it "jump in the pan." But I include *quick* in the title to emphasize the importance of just barely cooking the zucchini: As soon as it begins to give off a little moisture, get the pan off the burner. The zucchini should be warm, but not too hot. You just want to unlock its flavor and help it meld with those of the almonds and oil.

Bradley on Cheese

Parmigiano-Reggiano is a cow's milk cheese with a lighter touch, while Pecorino Romano is a sheep's milk cheese that works well with larger, lustier flavors. I don't consider them interchangeable. For this sauté, I prefer the robust character of Pecorino.

SERVES 4

¼ cup extra-virgin olive oil, plus more for serving

¼ cup sliced almonds

3 to 4 small zucchini, sliced lengthwise into ⅛-inch-thick slices, then crosswise into matchsticks (about 5 cups)

Salt and freshly ground black pepper

4 ounces Pecorino Romano, thinly sliced into 12 triangular sheets with an old-fashioned cheese slicer or very sharp knife, or shaved into shards with a vegetable peeler

Divide the oil among 2 large, heavy-bottomed skillets and heat it over high heat. When the oil is hot but not smoking, add half of the almonds to each pan. Cook, tossing or stirring, until the almonds are golden brown, approximately 30 seconds. Add half of the zucchini to each pan and toss or stir to coat the zucchini with the hot oil, just a few seconds. Remove the pans from the heat, season with salt and pepper, and return to the heat for 30 seconds, tossing to distribute the seasoning.

Divide the zucchini and almonds among 4 warm salad plates, drizzle with extra-virgin olive oil, arrange the Pecorino sheets in a pyramid over each serving, and get it to the table while it's still nice and hot.

Halibut with Grapefruit, Parsley, Red Onion, and Shiitake Mushrooms

Grapefruit on the dinner table? That's right. The sweet and tangy ruby red brings together earth (mushrooms) and sea (halibut) in this dish, with the flavors rounded out by the cream in the sauce, the sharpness of the red onion, and the herbaceous parsley, which gives the dish a nice lift.

SERVES 4

1½ large pink grapefruits

¾ cup torn parsley

¼ medium red onion, very thinly sliced

1 tablespoon extra-virgin olive oil

Salt

Freshly ground black pepper

1 tablespoon cream

8 tablespoons (1 stick) butter, cut into 8 pieces

Dash of hot sauce

½ cup canola oil

10 ounces shiitake mushrooms, caps only, thinly sliced (2 cups)

4 skinless halibut fillets, 6 ounces each

SECTION THE GRAPEFRUIT: Peel it by hand, then run a sharp, flexible knife blade over the surface of the fruit to remove as much pith as possible without cutting into the flesh. Separate the grapefruit into sections, then carefully remove the skin from 12 sections with the aid of a paring knife. Finally, remove and discard the seeds. Set the peeled sections aside. Squeeze ½ cup juice from the remaining sections, catching any seeds in your hands and discarding them.

To make the salad, put the grapefruit sections, parsley, onion, and extra-virgin olive oil in a bowl, season with salt and pepper, and very gently toss. Set aside.

To make the sauce, pour the grapefruit juice into a nonreactive saucepan and bring to a boil over high heat. Let boil until reduced to a glaze,

approximately 5 minutes. Whisk in the cream and let reduce for 1 minute. Remove the pan from the heat and whisk in the butter, 1 piece at a time. Whisk in a dash of hot sauce and season to taste with salt and pepper. Cover and set aside.

Heat ¼ cup of the canola oil in a sauté pan over medium heat. Add the mushrooms and sauté until they begin to crisp, approximately 4 minutes. Season with salt and pepper and set aside, covered, to keep warm.

Heat the remaining ¼ cup canola oil in a sauté pan set over medium-high heat. Season the fillets with salt and pepper and add them, skinned side up, to the pan. Sear for 3 to 4 minutes. Turn the fish over and cook for another 3 minutes. (To check for doneness, you can use a sharp, thin-bladed knife and apply slight pressure to peek between the fish's flakes and confirm that the flesh is opaque.)

Spoon some mushrooms onto the center of each of 4 dinner plates. Top with some salad, then a halibut fillet. Spoon the sauce around the mushrooms, and serve.

best of the best exclusive
Scallop Fritters

6 SERVINGS

Vegetable oil, for frying

½ cup all-purpose flour

½ cup yellow cornmeal

2 teaspoons baking powder

1¼ teaspoons kosher salt

Freshly ground pepper

2 large eggs, lightly beaten

¼ cup bottled clam broth

¼ cup pilsner beer

½ pound sea scallops, coarsely chopped

3 scallions, white and green parts, thinly sliced

¼ cup finely chopped red onion

1 small jalapeño with seeds, minced

Tartar sauce and lemon wedges, for serving

1. In a large saucepan, heat 2 inches of vegetable oil to 350°. Meanwhile, in a medium bowl, whisk the all-purpose flour with the cornmeal, baking powder, salt and a pinch of pepper. Add the eggs, clam broth and beer and whisk until the batter is smooth. Fold in the scallops, scallions, onion and jalapeño.

2. Working in batches, drop heaping teaspoons of the batter into the oil and fry, turning occasionally, until golden brown all over, about 7 minutes. Using a slotted spoon, transfer the fritters to paper towels to drain. Serve immediately with tartar sauce and lemon wedges.

Editor's Note

Cornmeal adds crunch to these fritters, which are reminiscent of the johnnycakes (cornmeal pancakes) of Bradley's native Rhode Island. You can substitute any firm fish or seafood, such as shrimp, cod, bay scallops or clams, in place of the sea scallops.

Maple Syrup Cookie Sandwiches
with Lemon Cream Filling, p. 62

Heirloom Baking with the Brass Sisters

By Marilynn Brass & Sheila Brass

Sisters Marilynn Brass and Sheila Brass own about 6,500 vintage cookbooks and 600 cooking molds. Their extensive collection of handwritten recipes from the 1890s to the 1970s—culled from their own kitchens, recipe boxes found at flea markets and even from an old manuscript salvaged from the town dump—inspired this baking book. "All these wonderful stories would have been lost," Marilynn says, "and now they're preserved." With its endearing anecdotes and photos, this is a lovely read as well as a terrific source for enticing desserts.

Published by Black Dog & Leventhal Publishers, $29.95.

Maple Syrup Cookie Sandwiches with Lemon Cream Filling
1930s

The Brass Sisters on Fillings

You can vary the filling for these cookies. Vanilla buttercream spiked with chopped candied ginger or Trappist ginger jam will also complement the maple flavor.

We were thrilled to find this handwritten recipe for a cookie made with maple syrup. We liked them so much we decided to pair them with a lemon cream filling, creating the gustatory opportunity to take them apart, lick the lemon cream and eat the cookies slowly to make them last. We found that it is easier to use a pastry bag to pipe and fill these cookies to insure that they are uniform in size and shape.

MAKES 60 COOKIES OR 30 FILLED SANDWICHES

FOR COOKIES

- 2 cups flour
- ½ teaspoon salt
- ½ teaspoon baking soda
- 1 cup maple syrup or cane syrup
- ½ cup butter
- 1 egg
- 2 teaspoons maple extract (optional)

FOR LEMON CREAM FILLING

- 2 cups confectioners' sugar
- ⅛ teaspoon salt
- ½ cup butter
- 3 teaspoons grated lemon zest
- 4 teaspoons lemon juice

1. Set the oven rack in the middle position. Preheat the oven to 350°F. Cover a 14-inch by 16-inch baking sheet with foil, shiny side up. Coat the foil with vegetable spray or use a silicone liner.

2. To make the cookies: Sift together flour, salt, and baking soda.

3. Mix maple syrup and butter in the bowl of a standing mixer fitted with the paddle attachment. Add egg and mix to combine. Gradually beat in sifted dry ingredients until the batter becomes smooth. Add maple extract.

4. Chill batter in the refrigerator until firm enough to pipe with a pastry bag. Fit pastry bag with a plain Ateco #804 metal tip and fill bag with batter. Pipe cookies onto baking sheet, making each cookie about 1½ inches in diameter and allowing no more than 20 cookies per sheet. Bake 18 minutes, or until golden brown. Place baking sheet on a rack. Let rest 2 minutes, then carefully transfer the cookies from baking sheet to rack. Cookies will crisp up on standing.

5. To make the lemon cream filling: Sift confectioners' sugar and salt into a small bowl. Add butter and combine. Whisk in lemon zest and lemon juice. Fit a pastry bag with an Ateco #806 metal tip and fill with lemon cream. Pipe a generous squiggle of filling on half of cookies. Place remaining cookies on top of filling and press together gently, sandwiching the cream in between. Store cookies between sheets of waxed paper in a covered tin in the refrigerator. Remove from refrigerator no more than 10 minutes before serving. This buttery filling will melt at room temperature.

Editor's Note

This recipe calls for piping the cookies, but if you prefer, you can use a tablespoon-size ice cream scoop to portion out the chilled batter evenly. The important thing is that the cookies are the same size so they can be easily sandwiched together.

Nell's Wonderful Peanut Butter Cookies

1930s

The Brass Sisters on Peanuts

We've discovered that using salted oiled peanuts lends a richness to these cookies that unsalted dry-roasted peanuts do not. If you do use unsalted dry-roasted peanuts, be sure to add ¼ teaspoon salt to the recipe.

This is a great simple recipe. That's all we can say about it. We used tasty salted oil-roasted peanuts. We found that the salt and the oil were essential to this full-flavored treat. We found this recipe jotted on the back of a bridge tally. Dare we say it's a winner?

MAKES 42 COOKIES

1¼ cups flour

½ teaspoon baking soda

½ teaspoon baking powder

½ cup butter

½ cup brown sugar

½ cup sugar

½ cup smooth peanut butter

 1 egg

½ cup broken salted peanuts (not dry-roasted)

½ cup mini chocolate chips

1. Set the oven rack in the middle position. Preheat the oven to 350°F. Cover a 14-inch by 16-inch baking sheet with foil, shiny side up. Coat the foil with vegetable spray or use a silicone liner.

2. Sift together flour, baking soda, and baking powder.

3. Cream butter, brown sugar, sugar, and peanut butter in the bowl of a standing mixer fitted with the paddle attachment. Add egg and mix thoroughly. Add sifted dry ingredients. Fold in peanuts and mini chocolate chips.

4. Chill dough in the refrigerator 1 hour, or until it is firm enough to handle. With floured hands or wearing disposable gloves, roll dough into balls about 1 inch in diameter. Place balls on baking sheet 2 inches apart and flatten with the bottom of a glass dipped in flour. Bake 12 minutes, or until golden brown. Cool on rack. Store between sheets of parchment paper or waxed paper in a covered tin.

Mrs. Carl Winchenbach's Banana Cream Pie
1940s

**The Brass Sisters'
Make-Ahead Tip**

We think this pie is good
for breakfast, lunch or
dinner. It can be made up
to one day ahead. Store
the pie loosely wrapped
in wax paper in a plastic
container in the fridge.

We think you should forget all you know about traditional banana cream pie
and start over with this recipe. We found it in a manuscript cookbook rescued
from the town dump. Mrs. Winchenbach lived in Waldoboro, Maine.

MAKES 8 TO 9 SLICES

9-inch pie shell, baked and cooled

 2 cups milk, divided

¼ cup light corn syrup

¼ cup cornstarch

½ cup sugar

¼ teaspoon salt

 3 egg yolks

 1 teaspoon vanilla

3 to 4 ripe bananas, sliced

1. Heat 1¾ cups of the milk and corn syrup in a heavy saucepan over
medium-low heat, stirring with a wooden spoon until bubbles start to
form around the edges, up to 7 minutes. Remove from heat.

2. Whisk together remaining ¼ cup milk and cornstarch in a bowl. Add sugar
and salt and mix thoroughly. Add egg yolks, one at a time, and whisk until
well blended. Add a little of the hot milk mixture to the egg mixture to temper
it, continuing to whisk briskly. Whisk remaining hot milk into eggs.

3. Return combined egg-milk mixture to saucepan. Bring to a simmer over
medium heat and cook, stirring continuously, about 30 seconds, or until
mixture begins to thicken (this will happen very quickly). Remove from heat,
whisk briefly, add vanilla, and whisk again.

4. Spread a small amount of custard on bottom of pie shell using an offset
spatula. Place a layer of sliced bananas on custard. Spread half of remaining
custard over bananas. Add remaining bananas and custard in layers. Cool
to room temperature and refrigerate until ready to serve. Decorate pie with
lightly sweetened whipped cream before serving.

Daddy's Bangor Brownies
1950s

There really was a Daddy: ours, Harry Brass, a hospital pharmacist, who
loved anything chocolate. How Daddy got involved with these brownies we
will never know. They are more cakey than fudgy, but we think they're
wonderful, and our mother baked them often for her bridge parties.

MAKES 48 SQUARES

1½ cups flour, sifted

 1 teaspoon salt

¾ cup butter

 1 cup brown sugar

 2 cups sugar

 6 eggs

 6 ounces bitter chocolate, melted and cooled

 2 teaspoons vanilla

¾ cup milk

 2 cups chopped walnuts

1. Set the oven rack in the middle position. Preheat the oven to 350°F. Line
the bottom and sides of a 9-inch by 13-inch by 2-inch pan with foil, shiny side
up, and coat with vegetable spray.

2. Sift together flour and salt.

3. Place butter, brown sugar, and sugar in the bowl of a standing mixer
fitted with the paddle attachment. Cream together until fluffy. Add eggs,
one at a time. Add chocolate. Add vanilla to milk. Add sifted dry ingredients
alternately with milk, beating after each addition. Fold in walnuts.

4. Pour batter into pan. Bake 30 to 35 minutes, or until tester inserted 1 inch
from edge comes out dry. (Tester inserted in center should come out with
moist crumbs.) Cool to room temperature and refrigerate until cold. Cut into
squares or triangles. Store between sheets of wax paper in a covered tin.

**The Brass Sisters
on Chocolate**
We use Hershey's, Nestlé
or Baker's chocolate
because these brands are
accessible. We have also
made this recipe with
fancier chocolate, and
there really isn't a huge
difference. Fancy chocolate
is great for eating on its
own but less significant
when you're baking with it.

Butterscotch Bars with Brown Sugar Meringue Topping
1930s

This is a delicious sweet bar. It's like two cookies in one, a bar cookie
and a brown sugar meringue. This Butterscotch Bar was very popular with
Midwestern ladies and their bridge clubs during the 1930s and 1940s.
Variations are still being exchanged at 21st-century bridge parties.

MAKES 40 BARS

FOR BARS

  2 cups pecan pieces

1½ cups flour

1½ teaspoons baking powder

 ⅛ teaspoon salt

  1 cup brown sugar

 ½ cup cold butter, cut into dice

  2 egg yolks

  1 teaspoon vanilla

FOR TOPPING

  2 egg whites

  1 cup brown sugar

1. Set the oven rack in the middle position. Preheat the oven to 350°F.
Line the bottom and sides of a 9-inch by 13-inch by 2-inch pan with foil,
shiny side up, and coat with vegetable spray. Line a 14-inch by 16-inch
baking sheet with foil.

2. To make the bars: Place pecan pieces on baking sheet. Toast in oven
7 to 10 minutes, stirring a few times for even browning. Do not allow
pecan pieces to burn. Cool to room temperature.

3. Combine flour, baking powder, salt, and brown sugar in the bowl of a
food processor fitted with a metal blade. Add butter. Process until butter
is the size of small peas. Add egg yolks and vanilla and pulse three
or four times until the mixture has the consistency of sandy clumps.

The Brass Sisters on Egg Whites

You can beat the whites for this meringue in a stand mixer, but if your mixer bowl is large it may be hard to do with such a small amount in the bowl. You can also use a hand mixer or just beat them with a whisk.

4. Pat mixture into pan and level off by pressing with a small offset spatula. Press pecans into mixture.

5. To make topping: Place egg whites in the bowl of a standing mixer fitted with the whisk attachment. Beat until whites hold a peak when the whisk is lifted. Add brown sugar and beat at highest speed about 4 minutes. Spread meringue over pecan layer. Bake 25 minutes, or until a tester inserted into bars comes out clean. The meringue will crack slightly, but this will not significantly affect the appearance. Let cool on rack completely and cut into squares. Store between sheets of wax paper in a covered tin.

best of the best exclusive

Toasted-Almond Butter Cookies

MAKES ABOUT 3 DOZEN COOKIES

⅓ cup slivered almonds

Vegetable oil cooking spray

1 cup plus 1½ tablespoons all-purpose flour, plus more for dusting

½ cup confectioners' sugar

¾ teaspoon finely grated lemon zest

⅛ teaspoon salt

1 stick plus 2 tablespoons cold unsalted butter, cut into ½-inch dice

1 large egg, separated

1. Preheat the oven to 350°. Spread the almonds in a pie plate and toast for about 6 minutes, until lightly golden; let cool. Line 2 large baking sheets with foil and coat lightly with cooking spray.

2. In a food processor, pulse the 1 cup plus 1½ tablespoons of flour with the confectioners' sugar, lemon zest and salt. Add the butter and pulse until crumbly. Add the egg yolk and pulse just until the dough comes together. Turn the dough out onto a floured work surface and gather into a ball. Flatten the dough into a disk and wrap in plastic. Refrigerate for 2 hours, or until firm.

3. Roll rounded teaspoons of the dough into balls and place on the prepared baking sheets. Using the bottom of a lightly floured glass, gently flatten the balls to a ¼-inch thickness. Brush the cookies with the egg white and top with the toasted almonds, pressing them in gently. Bake for 18 minutes or until the edges and bottoms of the cookies are golden. Let cool on the baking sheets for 5 minutes, then transfer the cookies to a rack to cool completely.

MAKE AHEAD The cookies can be stored in an airtight container for up to 3 days.

Editor's Note

The Brass sisters found the recipe for this butter cookie in a typewritten cookbook manuscript from the 1930s. They think the recipes, which have an Austrian flavor, must have been handed down over generations before being collected and typed.

A view of the Tyrrhenian coast in Biba's beloved Italy.

Biba's Italy

By Biba Caggiano

In this charming cookbook, star California chef Biba Caggiano provides straightforward, rustic recipes for traditional dishes from her five favorite Italian cities—Rome, Florence, Milan, Bologna and Venice—as well as lively descriptions of her most beloved *osterias, enotecas,* markets and shops in each place. With Caggiano as their excellent guide, home cooks can not only make the quintessential Chicken with Peppers alla Romana, they'll also know the best place to eat it (Trattoria Sabatini) the next time they are visiting Rome.

Published by Artisan, $29.95.

Chicken with Peppers alla Romana

Pollo con Peperoni

Caggiano on Tomatoes

Use fresh tomatoes in this recipe when they're in season. Blanch them in boiling water for a few minutes, then peel off their skins and break them up a little. Out of season, canned San Marzano tomatoes are the best. They come from an area in Naples with fabulous weather and soil for tomatoes. And they're picked and packed really ripe—you can see it right away when you open the can.

SERVES 4

½ cup extra-virgin olive oil

1 large plump chicken (4 to 5 pounds), cut into 8 serving pieces, thoroughly washed and patted dry with paper towels

1 teaspoon salt plus more to taste

¼ teaspoon freshly ground black pepper plus more to taste

1 garlic clove, minced

2 to 3 ounces thickly sliced prosciutto, diced

1 cup dry white wine

1 (28-ounce) can Italian plum tomatoes, preferably San Marzano, coarsely chopped, with their juices

4 large green, red, or yellow bell peppers (preferably a mixture of all colors), washed, seeded, and cut into 1-inch strips

Heat half of the oil in a large skillet over medium-high heat. Add the chicken and cook, turning the pieces to brown on all sides, about 8 minutes. Season with salt and pepper.

Add the garlic and the prosciutto, and stir for about 1 minute. Add the wine and cook, stirring and moving the chicken pieces around, until the wine is almost all evaporated, 5 to 6 minutes. Add the chopped tomatoes and their juices and bring to a boil. Reduce the heat to low, partially cover the pan, and simmer very gently, stirring and basting the chicken from time to time, for about 30 minutes.

Meanwhile, heat the remaining oil in another large skillet over medium-high heat. Add the peppers and cook, stirring, until they begin to soften and their skin is somewhat charred, 8 to 10 minutes.

Scoop up the peppers with a large slotted spoon or tongs and add to the chicken. Simmer gently, stirring occasionally, until the meat is tender and the sauce has a rich brown color and a medium-thick consistency, 8 to 10 minutes. Taste, adjust the seasoning, and serve. (The whole dish can be prepared a few hours ahead. Reheat gently before serving.)

Pan-Fried Zucchini with Vinegar and Chili Pepper
Zucchine in Padella con Aceto e Peperoncino

Fried zucchini are popular all over Italy, and change little from area to area. In Rome this appetizing dish is given extra flavor by the addition of *peperoncino* (small, red chili pepper) and crushed garlic that browns in the oil and infuses it with its aroma before being discarded. The last-minute splash of vinegar rounds up all the flavors. It can be served as an appetizer, or it makes an especially good side dish with grilled meat or fish.

SERVES 4

¼ cup extra-virgin olive oil

2 large garlic cloves, peeled and lightly crushed

1½ pounds zucchini, the smallest you can find, washed, dried, ends trimmed, and cut into ¼-inch-thick rounds

Salt to taste

1 small red *peperoncino*, finely shredded, or crushed red pepper flakes to taste

2 to 3 tablespoons red-wine vinegar

1 tablespoon chopped fresh flat-leaf parsley

Heat the oil in a large frying pan or skillet over medium-high heat. When the oil is hot but not yet smoking, add the garlic and cook until golden brown on both sides, 2 to 3 minutes. Discard the garlic. Add the zucchini without crowding (fry in 2 batches if needed) and cook, stirring and turning the zucchini until golden brown on both sides, about 2 minutes.

Season with salt and the *peperoncino* or pepper flakes. Add the vinegar and stir until almost all evaporated, 1 to 2 minutes. Stir in the parsley, taste, and adjust the seasoning. Serve warm or at room temperature.

Editor's Note

Try this flexible recipe with other quick-cooking vegetables like green beans, or blanch longer-cooking vegetables like cauliflower or winter squash before substituting them for the zucchini.

Poached Salmon with Bolognese Salsa Verde

Salmone Lesso con Salsa Verde Bolognese

Caggiano on Salsa Verde

Salsa verde is a parsley and olive oil sauce with a very piquant, wonderfully fresh taste. In Bologna, where I grew up, it is traditionally served with *bollito misto,* a combination of meats like chicken, capon, brisket, pork, sausage and beef tongue that is boiled very slowly for several hours.

On a hot summer day, there is no food that pleases me more than a perfectly grilled, roasted, poached, or steamed fish, topped simply by a bit of green olive oil and a few drops of lemon juice. Such a fish dish is typical of good home cooking and of the many unpretentious restaurants and trattorie of Bologna such as Diana, Rodrigo, Battibecco, and Cesari.

SERVES 4

FOR THE SALSA VERDE

Yolks of 2 hard-boiled eggs

2 loosely packed cups fresh flat-leaf parsley, washed and dried well

1 tablespoon capers, rinsed

1 garlic clove, peeled

4 anchovy fillets

3 small pickled gherkins, drained and cut into large pieces

2 small cipolline onions pickled in wine vinegar, rinsed (optional)

1 teaspoon Dijon mustard

1 teaspoon grated lemon zest and juice of 1 lemon

½ cup extra-virgin olive oil, or more if needed

Salt to taste

FOR THE SALMON

1 cup dry white wine

1 medium carrot, cut into 1-inch pieces

½ small onion, peeled and quartered

1 celery stalk, cut into 1-inch pieces

1 tablespoon black peppercorns

4 sprigs of fresh flat-leaf parsley

Salt to taste

4 salmon fillets, each 1 inch thick (about 8 ounces each)

Olive oil, for drizzling

1 lemon, cut into wedges

PREPARE THE SALSA VERDE

Put all the ingredients except the lemon juice, oil, and salt in the bowl of a food processor fitted with the metal blade. Pulse until the ingredients are finely chopped but not puréed. Transfer to a bowl. Add the lemon juice and oil and stir energetically to blend; the sauce should have a medium-thick consistency and a slightly piquant taste. Add a bit of salt and more oil, if needed. Cover the bowl and refrigerate. Salsa verde can be refrigerated up to 3 days. Bring to room temperature before serving.

PREPARE THE SALMON

Fill a large skillet halfway with water. Add the wine, carrot, onion, celery, peppercorns, parsley, and salt. Bring to a boil, reduce the heat to medium low, and simmer for about 30 minutes.

Slip the salmon into the pan without overlapping, making sure that each piece is completely covered by the broth (add a bit of water if needed). As soon as the broth comes back to a boil, reduce the heat to low and simmer gently for 4 to 5 minutes. Turn off the heat and let the salmon sit in the flavorful broth until its inside is no longer translucent, 6 to 7 minutes longer.

Pick up the salmon with a large metal spatula, pat dry with paper towels, and place on serving plates. Season with salt to taste, drizzle with olive oil and lemon juice, and serve with a couple tablespoons of salsa verde.

NOTE If you prefer serving chilled salmon, leave the salmon in its broth and place it in the refrigerator for several hours or overnight. It will be incredibly moist and flavorful.

Rigatoni Dragged with Florentine Meat Ragù

Rigatoni Strascicati col Ragù

Editor's Note

Chicken livers make this meat sauce special, adding deep flavor and rich body. If you don't like liver, just leave it out—it won't be an authentic Florentine ragù, but it will still be delicious.

SERVES 6

FOR THE RAGÙ

⅓ cup extra-virgin olive oil

1 small onion, finely minced (about 1 cup)

1 small carrot, minced (about ½ cup)

1 small celery stalk, minced (about ½ cup)

1 small sprig of fresh rosemary leaves, chopped (about 2 tablespoons)

1 tablespoon chopped fresh flat-leaf parsley

2 garlic cloves, peeled and minced

1 pound ground beef chuck

3 to 4 chicken livers, finely minced

1 cup medium-bodied red wine, such as Chianti Classico

2 large ripe tomatoes, or 3 canned plum tomatoes, peeled and minced

⅛ teaspoon freshly grated nutmeg

Small pinch of crushed red pepper flakes

Grated zest of ½ lemon

Salt to taste

2½ cups Chicken Broth (recipe follows) or canned low-sodium broth

TO COMPLETE THE DISH

1 tablespoon coarse salt

1 pound dried rigatoni or penne

1 to 2 tablespoons unsalted butter

½ cup freshly grated Parmigiano-Reggiano

PREPARE THE RAGÙ

Heat the oil in a medium saucepan over medium heat. As soon as the oil is nice and hot, add the onion, carrot, and celery, and cook, stirring, until the vegetables begin to soften, about 5 minutes. Add the rosemary, parsley, and garlic, and stir until the mixture has a nice golden color, 3 to 4 minutes more.

Raise the heat to high. Add the beef and the chicken livers and cook, stirring from time to time and breaking up the meat with a wooden spoon, until the meat is golden brown, 10 to 12 minutes.

Add the wine and stir until half of it has evaporated. Add the tomatoes, nutmeg, red pepper flakes, and lemon zest. Season with salt. Add 2 cups of the chicken broth and bring to a fast simmer. Reduce the heat to very low, partially cover, and simmer, stirring from time to time, until the ragù has a rich brown color and dense consistency, about 2 hours. If the sauce reduces too much, add a little more broth. Taste, adjust the seasoning, and set aside until ready to use. The ragù can be prepared several hours or a few days ahead.

FINISH THE DISH

Bring a large pot of water to a boil over high heat. Add the coarse salt and the rigatoni and cook, stirring occasionally with a wooden spoon, until the pasta is tender but still firm to the bite. Scoop up and reserve 1 cup of the cooking water.

Meanwhile, reheat the ragù in a large skillet over medium heat. Drain the pasta and place it in the skillet with the ragù. Add the butter and about half of the Parmigiano and stir, dragging the pasta and the sauce together to combine. (Add just a little of the reserved pasta water if the sauce seems too dry.) Taste, adjust the seasoning, and serve with the remaining Parmigiano.

Caggiano on Pasta
I use rigatoni for this dish because the sauce is nice and thick and the ridged pasta absorbs it very well.

Chicken Broth

MAKES ABOUT 4 QUARTS

- 1 (4-pound) stewing chicken or boiling hen
- 3 pounds bones and meat scraps from veal and chicken
- 1 large yellow onion, peeled and quartered
- 2 carrots, cut into large pieces
- 2 celery stalks, cut into large pieces
- 1 canned Italian plum tomato

Salt to taste

Wash the meats and the vegetables, except the tomato, well under cold running water. Put everything except the salt in a large stockpot and cover by 2 to 3 inches with cold water. Set the cover askew and bring to a gentle boil over medium heat. As soon as the water begins to bubble, reduce the heat to low. With a slotted spoon or a skimmer, skim off the foam that has risen to the surface. Cover the pot partially and cook at the gentlest of simmers for 2½ to 3 hours, skimming off the foam every 20 to 30 minutes. Season with salt during the last few minutes of cooking.

Remove the meats and set aside. If using the broth right away, strain it through a fine-mesh strainer directly into another pot. If using within a few days, strain it into a metal bowl and set it over a larger bowl filled with ice water until cool. Refrigerate the broth for a day or two, or freeze it. Before using, remove the fat that has solidified on the surface.

best of the best exclusive

Braised Pork and Cabbage Salad

4 SERVINGS

Two 1½-pound pork shanks or 3 pounds bone-in pork shoulder

1 yellow onion, quartered

1 carrot, cut into 1-inch lengths

1 celery rib, cut into 1-inch lengths

1 sprig flat-leaf parsley

1 tablespoon Dijon mustard

¼ cup red wine vinegar

¾ cup extra-virgin olive oil

Kosher salt and freshly ground pepper

1 small head of Savoy cabbage (about 1½ pounds), finely shredded

½ small red onion, thinly sliced

¼ cup plus ½ tablespoon capers, drained and rinsed

1. In a large saucepan, combine the pork, yellow onion, carrot, celery and parsley. Add enough water to submerge the pork. Cover and simmer over moderately low heat for 2½ hours, or until very tender. Remove from the heat and let the pork cool in its liquid, about 2 hours.

2. Meanwhile, in a small bowl, whisk the mustard with the vinegar. Whisk in the olive oil and season the dressing with salt and pepper.

3. In a large bowl, toss the cabbage with the red onion, capers and ¾ cup of the dressing and season with salt and pepper. Let stand at room temperature for 1 hour.

4. Shred the pork, discarding all of the bones and fat. Add the pork to the cabbage salad and toss well. Transfer the salad to plates and pass the remaining dressing at the table.

MAKE AHEAD The pork can be refrigerated in its cooking liquid for up to 3 days. Reheat gently before shredding.

Editor's Note

Caggiano uses pork shanks here, which you can order from a butcher, but we found the recipe worked equally well with pork shoulder. Save the cooking liquid to use in soups or rich sauces that call for pork stock.

Chorizo and Chickpea
One-Pot Supper, p. 84

The Food of Northern Spain

By Jenny Chandler

"In Spain, food is simply an excuse to get together," says Jenny Chandler, whose first cookbook tackles the diverse dishes of the country's northern regions. "Sixteen people sitting around a table on the weekend, that sort of thing still exists there." Her book focuses on the dishes that anchor these gatherings—from fast, hearty Chorizo and Chickpea One-Pot Supper to sweet-savory Corn Cakes with Cabrales Blue Cheese and Honey—organized loosely by course and accompanied by bits of fascinating local lore and engaging personal anecdotes.

Published by Pavilion Books, $35.

Chorizo and Chickpea One-Pot Supper

Potaje de Chorizo y Garbanzos

SERVES 4–6

2 tablespoons olive oil

2 onions, diced

2 garlic cloves, diced

9 ounces chorizo, hot or sweet, sliced

1 pound 8 ounces canned chickpeas

14 ounces canned chopped plum tomatoes

2 tablespoons sultanas (golden raisins)

Juice of ½ lemon

Salt and freshly ground black pepper

1 tablespoon toasted pine kernels (pine nuts)

1 tablespoon roughly chopped fresh flat-leaf parsley

Drizzle of extra virgin olive oil

Heat the olive oil in a large frying pan (skillet). Add the onions and fry until they are soft, then add the garlic and chorizo.

Once the pan is swirling with the smoky, red chorizo fat, add the chickpeas, stirring to cover them in the delicious oil.

Add the tomatoes and sultanas (golden raisins) and cook until heated through.

Taste—I usually find that the chickpeas need a little lemon juice to liven them and a bit of salt and pepper.

Sprinkle with pine kernels (pine nuts), parsley and a dash of olive oil.

VARIATIONS

Fresh spinach is great stirred in with the tomatoes and just allowed to wilt.

Morcilla, black pudding (blood sausage), could replace the chorizo or you could use a mixture of the two.

El Bierzo roasted peppers could be added straight from the jar or you could roast your own (bell) peppers and throw them in.

Spinach with Pine Kernels and Sultanas

Espinacas con Pasas y Piñones

This is an ancient recipe that pops up all around the Mediterranean; it is equally good made with Swiss chard. You could add a little ham or bacon too if you like.

I remember spending hours as a teenage au pair combing the ground below the umbrella pines for nuts. It was the daily post-siesta challenge with my toddler charges; we rarely managed more than a fistful of pine kernels (pine nuts) and they certainly never made it as far as the kitchen.

SERVES 4

- 2 pounds 4 ounces fresh young spinach, washed
- 3 tablespoons olive oil
- 1 ounce or ⅛ cup pine kernels (pine nuts)
- 1 ounce or ⅛ cup sultanas (golden raisins), soaked in warm water for 30 minutes

Salt and freshly ground black pepper

Place the spinach in a large saucepan with a tightly fitting lid; you will not need to add any more water if the spinach is still damp from washing, otherwise a splash will do. Cook the spinach over a medium heat until it has wilted, you may want to give it a stir after a couple of minutes. Drain the spinach; oh and do save the juice, it makes a delicious drink. Chop the spinach roughly.

Heat the olive oil in a frying pan. Add the pine kernels (pine nuts) and fry until they begin to brown, then add the spinach and sultanas (golden raisins). Toss everything in the oil and heat through. Taste for salt and pepper and serve.

Chandler on Spinach Juice
I horrify people who come to my cooking classes by insisting they save the water in the bottom of the pan after cooking spinach. It's full of goodness, so I can't bear to see it poured down the sink. Drink It or tip it into your next stew.

Corn Cakes with Cabrales Blue Cheese and Honey

Tortos de Maís con Queso Cabrales y Miel

Editor's Note

Spanish heather honey is a full-flavored honey with a rich amber color. For this recipe, any all-purpose honey, such as orange blossom or wildflower, will add a contrasting sweetness to the tangy cheese. You can order heather honey from La Tienda (800-710-4304 or tienda.com).

Corn once played a vital role in the peasant diet of northwestern Spain. Introduced from America, it flourished here and the countryside of Asturias and Galicia is still studded with *horréos* or granaries. These small buildings on pillars were built to store and protect the cobs. Corn bread and *tortos* were absolute staples, later superseded by wheat bread.

I came across these tiny corn cakes in the village of Asiegu, high in the Asturian Picos de Europa. The views are apparently quite stunning, not that I saw them as we were engulfed in a thick Atlantic fog. I drowned my sorrows with some homemade cider and these tasty corn cakes topped with the local Cabrales blue cheese and heather honey from the mountainside.

SERVES 4 (MAKES ABOUT 12 SMALL TORTOS)

- 4 ounces cornmeal, *masa harina* or polenta (the polenta processed in a blender until fine and soft)
- 1 ounce or ¼ cup all-purpose flour
- 1 teaspoon salt
- ½ cup boiling water
- Olive oil, for frying
- 7 ounces Cabrales, Picos de Europa or Roquefort cheese
- 6 tablespoons runny heather honey

Place the cornmeal, flour and salt in a bowl. Pour the boiling water over the flour and stir with a wooden spoon until the mixture is a doughy consistency. You may need a couple of extra tablespoons of water. Leave to cool.

Once cool enough, roll the dough into walnut-sized balls and lay them on a damp cloth. With dampened hands, flatten them to about ½ inch thick. You should finish up with about 12 small disks.

Heat the olive oil in a frying pan (skillet). Add the *tortos* and fry until they are completely golden and cooked through. Drain well on paper towels, then top each cake with a little Cabrales cheese and a drizzle of honey. Serve at once, otherwise the corn cakes will become tough and rubbery.

Spinach, Cured Ham and Goat's Cheese Salad with a Hazelnut and Honey Dressing

Ensalada de Espinacas Tiernas, Jamón y Queso de Cabra

Editor's Note

Serrano ham is a dry-cured Spanish ham that's aged for over a year, developing a rich, nutty flavor. The closest substitute is Italian prosciutto, which will also work well in this salad.

SERVES 4 AS A STARTER (APPETIZER) OR 2–3 AS A MAIN COURSE

4 thin slices of *jamón serrano*

Oil, for oiling

7 ounces or 4⅜ cups baby spinach leaves

12 ripe cherry tomatoes, quartered

6 sun-dried tomatoes, finely chopped

5 ounces fresh soft goat's cheese, cut into small chunks

FOR THE DRESSING

1 tablespoon honey

5 tablespoons extra virgin olive oil

Juice of ½ lemon

Salt and freshly ground black pepper

1 ounce or ¼ cup toasted hazelnuts, roughly chopped

Preheat the oven to 325°F.

Place the *jamón* on a lightly oiled baking tray (cookie sheet) and cook in the oven for 10 minutes, then leave to cool and crispen. The ham should be really brittle as it cools; if not, just return it to the oven for a few more minutes.

Meanwhile, place all the dressing ingredients in a screw-top jar or container with a tight-fitting lid. Give the jar a good shake, then taste. You may need to adjust the quantities. It can be quite sweet since the *jamón,* sun-dried tomatoes and cheese are quite salty (if you are making the dressing ahead of time, just add the hazelnuts at the last minute so they keep their crunch).

Next, combine the spinach leaves with the cherry and sun-dried tomatoes, add most of the dressing and toss together.

Break the crispy *jamón* into bite-sized pieces and sprinkle these over the salad with the goat's cheese. Drizzle over the remaining vinaigrette and serve.

best of the best exclusive
Catalan Chicken

Editor's Note

Though all the ingredients here are cooked together in one casserole, the pieces of dried fruit can be served as a sweet, chunky side dish for the chicken. This is wonderful over couscous, accompanied by a crisp salad or sautéed greens.

6 SERVINGS

⅔   cup dried apricots
½   cup golden raisins
¼   cup brandy
 2   tomatoes, halved
 3   tablespoons extra-virgin olive oil
 6   whole chicken legs (4½ pounds)
Kosher salt and freshly ground pepper
½   pound thickly sliced bacon, cut into ½-inch pieces
 2   large onions, cut into ¼-inch dice
 1   head of garlic, cloves peeled
½   cup dry white wine
 3   thyme sprigs
 1   bay leaf
2½ cups chicken stock or low-sodium broth
¼   cup pine nuts

1. In a small bowl, toss the apricots and raisins with the brandy. Let stand for 30 minutes.

2. Preheat the oven to 400°F. Grate the cut side of the tomatoes on a box grater set over a bowl. Discard the tomato skins.

3. In a large cast-iron casserole, heat the olive oil until shimmering. Season the chicken legs with salt and pepper. Add 3 legs to the casserole and cook over moderately high heat, turning once, until browned, 10 minutes. Transfer to a plate. Repeat with the remaining 3 legs. Pour off the fat from the casserole.

4. Add the bacon to the casserole and cook over moderate heat until browned, about 6 minutes. Spoon off all but 3 tablespoons of the fat from the casserole. Add the onions and garlic cloves to the bacon and cook until the onions begin to brown, about 6 minutes. Stir in the dried-fruit mixture, tomatoes, wine, thyme sprigs and bay leaf and boil over high heat for 1 minute. Pour in the chicken stock.

5. Return the chicken legs to the casserole, skin side up, and bring to a boil. Transfer the casserole to the oven and bake until the chicken is cooked through and the sauce has thickened, about 40 minutes. Discard the thyme sprigs and bay leaf.

6. Meanwhile, in a small, dry skillet, toast the pine nuts over moderate heat, stirring frequently, until fragrant and lightly golden, about 3 minutes.

7. Transfer the chicken to a platter. Spoon the sauce around the chicken, sprinkle with the toasted pine nuts and serve.

Pollo Frito, p. 94

Giada's Family Dinners

By *Giada De Laurentiis*

Giada De Laurentiis became a Food Network star in part because she seems eminently approachable. Her latest book is that way, too: "Reading this book is like flipping through my family scrapbook," she says. "Many of the recipes are those we've served at gatherings for years." De Laurentiis likes to keep her food simple and unpretentious. For instance, her super-quick and ingenious Salami Crisps with Sour Cream and Basil call for only three ingredients, and she makes her Gorgonzola and tomato pizzettes with store-bought pizza dough.

Published by Clarkson Potter, $32.50.
Find more recipes by Giada De Laurentiis at foodandwine.com/delaurentiis

Pollo Frito

Editor's Note

Lemon juice and olive oil not only add flavor to the Pollo Frito, but also tenderize the chicken and help keep it moist. We found the chicken was best when marinated for 1 to 4 hours.

Everybody loves fried chicken, and my family and I are no exceptions. The lemon juice is the secret ingredient to the fresh flavor in this crispy dish. In southern Italy lemons are abundant and are used in everything.

4 SERVINGS

¼ cup fresh lemon juice (from about 2 lemons)

¼ cup extra-virgin olive oil

1½ teaspoons salt

1 teaspoon freshly ground black pepper

1 (3½-pound) frying chicken, cut into 8 serving pieces

Approximately 2 cups olive oil, for frying

1 cup all-purpose flour

Lemon wedges

In a large resealable plastic bag, combine the lemon juice, extra-virgin olive oil, salt, and pepper. Add the chicken pieces and seal the bag. Gently shake the bag to ensure the chicken is coated with the marinade. Refrigerate for at least 2 hours and up to 1 day, turning the bag occasionally.

Preheat the oven to 200°F. In a large cast-iron frying pan or other heavy frying pan, add enough oil to come ⅓ inch up the sides of the pan. Heat the oil over medium heat. Meanwhile, drain the marinade from the chicken and pat the chicken dry with paper towels. Dredge half of the chicken pieces in the flour to coat completely; shake off the excess flour. Add the coated chicken to the hot oil and fry until it is golden brown and just cooked through, turning occasionally, about 25 minutes. Using tongs, transfer the chicken to a paper towel–lined plate to drain the excess oil. Then place the fried chicken on a baking sheet and keep it warm in the oven while frying the remaining chicken. Repeat coating and frying the remaining chicken.

Arrange the fried chicken on a warm platter and serve with the lemon wedges.

Salami Crisps with Sour Cream and Basil

Every time I make these for a party they absolutely disappear. If you like beef jerky you will *love* these. The recipe is easy to double or even triple for a big crowd and can be made ahead of time, too.

MAKES 24 PIECES

24 thin slices Italian dry salami (about 4 ounces)

⅓ cup sour cream

3 tablespoons thinly sliced fresh basil leaves

Preheat the oven to 325°F. Line 2 heavy large baking sheets with aluminum foil. Arrange the salami in a single layer over the baking sheets. Bake until the salami slices are amber brown, watching closely to ensure they brown evenly, about 10 minutes. Transfer the salami crisps to a paper towel–lined baking sheet to absorb the excess oil. Set aside to cool. (The salami crisps can be made 8 hours ahead. Store at room temperature in an airtight container.)

Spoon a dollop of sour cream onto each salami crisp. Sprinkle with the basil and serve.

Editor's Note

Quick and flavorful, these salami crisps are a great way to add crunch to a recipe. Make extra and crumble them over salads, soups or pasta.

Pizzettes with Gorgonzola, Tomato, and Basil

De Laurentiis on Toppings

De Laurentiis on Toppings

Those little bits of leftover cheese, cooked beans, cured meats or veggies you've got in the fridge make great toppings for *pizzettes.* My only rule is not to load on too much or combine too many flavors; you should be able to taste the dough, and each ingredient, in every bite.

Pizzettes are bite-size pizzas, and you can top them with any of your favorite pizza toppings. This is a bit of a variation on the classic *margherita*—I find the Gorgonzola and sweet cherry tomatoes make a great appetite enhancer. Other combos to try are grated fontina cheese, chopped mushrooms, and prosciutto, or coarse sea salt, extra-virgin olive oil, and fresh rosemary.

8 TO 10 SERVINGS

- 1 ball (12 ounces) purchased pizza dough
- 5 ounces Gorgonzola cheese, crumbled
- 5 ounces cherry tomatoes, quartered
- 1 tablespoon extra-virgin olive oil
- ⅓ cup fresh basil leaves, torn into pieces

Salt and freshly ground black pepper

Preheat the oven to 475°F. Roll out the pizza dough into a ¼-inch-thick round. Using a 2¼- to 2½-inch-diameter cookie cutter, cut out 30 dough circles. Arrange the circles on 2 large, heavy baking sheets. Sprinkle the Gorgonzola cheese over the circles. Top with the tomatoes, pressing them gently into the dough. Bake until the *pizzettes* are golden brown, about 10 minutes. Drizzle the *pizzettes* with the oil, then sprinkle with the basil, salt, and pepper. Arrange the *pizzettes* on a platter and serve immediately.

Date-Night Chicken, p. 100

How to Boil Water

By Food Network Kitchens

"Everyone starts out *not* cooking," says Katherine Alford, coauthor of this cookbook aimed at novices. Beginning with the assumption that the reader has minimal to no kitchen skills, each recipe provides detailed directions and photos showing nearly every step. In addition to basic technique tips like how to chop an onion and boil an egg, the book includes both standards like meat loaf and mashed potatoes, and such inventive recipes as Mexican Fish & Chips and Southeast Asian–Style Beef Salad—dishes that appeal to cooks at all levels.

Published by Meredith Books, $24.95.

Date-Night Chicken

SERVES 2 TO 4 • PREP TIME: 1 HOUR 30 MINUTES

8 cloves garlic

1 medium onion

¾ cup pitted dates

¾ cup pitted green olives

1 lemon

3 tablespoons extra-virgin olive oil

1 bay leaf

2 teaspoons kosher salt, plus more for seasoning

Freshly ground black pepper

1 chicken, quartered (about 3 to 4 pounds)

1 teaspoon ground cumin

2 to 3 tablespoons chicken broth or water

Handful fresh parsley or cilantro leaves (optional)

Couscous, for serving

1. Preheat oven to 400°F. Smash and peel the garlic cloves and put into a shallow baking dish or casserole. Halve and thinly slice the onion. Quarter the dates and add them to the dish. Scatter the olives on top.

2. Peel 6 long strips of zest from the lemon with a vegetable peeler, add to the dish, then juice lemon over the top. Toss everything with half of the olive oil, the bay leaf, the 2 teaspoons salt and some black pepper.

3. Put the chicken quarters, skin side up, on top of the onion mixture, brush with the remaining olive oil, and season with the cumin, some salt, and some black pepper. Bake until the chicken is golden brown and the onion mixture is tender and juicy, about 1 hour and 15 minutes.

4. Transfer the chicken to a serving platter, discard the bay leaf and stir the broth or water into the onions, dates, and olives to glaze them. Spoon the goodies around and on the chicken. Rinse and chop the parsley, if using, and scatter over the top. Serve with couscous.

Mexican Fish & Chips

SERVES 4 • PREP TIME: 30 MINUTES

- 2 tablespoons extra-virgin olive oil
- 1 7-ounce can salsa verde (tomatillo salsa) (about ¾ cup)
- 3 scallions

Large handful tortilla chips

- ½ cup crumbled feta cheese (see Make It Your Own)
- 4 6-ounce skinless mahimahi or grouper fillets

Kosher salt and freshly ground black pepper

Handful fresh cilantro

1. Preheat the oven to 450°F. Heat 1 tablespoon of the olive oil in a medium skillet over medium-high heat. Add the salsa and cook, stirring, until thickened, about 3 minutes. Pour salsa into a 9x13-inch baking dish and cool slightly.

2. Slice the scallions. Crumble the tortilla chips by hand in a medium bowl to yield about ⅔ cup. Mix with the scallions, cheese, and remaining tablespoon olive oil.

3. Lightly season each fish fillet with some salt and black pepper. Turn fish in the salsa to coat and arrange, skinned side down, in the pan. Pat the chip mixture evenly on top of fish.

4. Bake until fish is opaque and topping is lightly browned, about 20 minutes. Chop cilantro, sprinkle over fish, and serve immediately.

UPGRADE

Sprinkle ¼ cup chopped green Spanish olives over the salsa verde.

MAKE IT YOUR OWN

If you can find it, try a Mexican cheese in place of feta. *Queso blanco* (fresh, firm, creamy), *queso fresco* (semisoft, salty, not too melty), or *cotija añejo* (crumbly, dry, strong) all work well here. Leftover *queso fresco* is excellent in quesadillas and burritos, or crumble *cotija* or *queso blanco* over soup or chili.

Food Network Kitchens on Crunchy Coatings

Many people find fish recipes intimidating, so we wanted to make them accessible. In this recipe, you can use crumbled tortilla chips from the bottom of the bag to create a crispy crust without frying. You can substitute chicken breasts for fish here, too.

Buffalo Chicken Sub Sandwiches

SERVES 4 • PREP TIME: 20 MINUTES

- 3 boneless, skin-on chicken breast halves (about 1½ pounds)
- 2 teaspoons chili powder
- Kosher salt and freshly ground black pepper
- 6 tablespoons unsalted butter
- 1 to 2 ribs celery
- ½ bunch watercress
- 1 baguette (a.k.a. French bread, 15 to 18 inches long)
- 4 tablespoons hot sauce
- 2 ounces creamy blue cheese, like Saga blue
- ¼ cup mayonnaise or sour cream

1. Preheat the oven to 350°F. Pat the chicken dry with paper towels and season all over with chili powder and some salt and black pepper. Heat a large skillet over medium-high heat; add 2 tablespoons of the butter. Lay the chicken skin side down in the skillet and cook without moving until the skin is golden and crispy, about 4 minutes. Turn and cook until the chicken is opaque, about 4 minutes more. Reserve the skillet. Put the chicken in a baking dish or roasting pan and bake until firm to the touch, about 10 minutes. Set chicken aside to rest for 5 minutes before slicing.

2. While the chicken bakes, thinly slice the celery. Trim and discard the tough stems from the watercress. Rinse, dry, and set aside the leaves.

3. Cut the bread crosswise into 4 equal pieces; cut each piece in half for sub-style sandwiches. Add 2 tablespoons butter to the reserved skillet. Once the butter stops foaming, toast half the bread, cut side down, pressing the pieces to soak up the butter, about 2 minutes. Transfer to a platter and brush with half the hot sauce. Repeat with the remaining butter, bread, and hot sauce.

4. Spread the cheese evenly on the bottoms of the bread. Layer the celery over the cheese. Thinly slice the chicken and place on the celery. Top with the watercress and smear the top pieces of bread with mayonnaise. Press the tops on the sandwiches and serve or wrap and serve within 2 hours.

Southeast Asian–Style Beef Salad

SERVES 4 • PREP TIME: 20 MINUTES

12 ounces flank steak (about half of a full one)

¾ cup Sriracha-Miso Dressing (recipe follows) or store-bought ginger-miso dressing

3 scallions

1 medium carrot

1 Kirby cucumber (see Shopsmart, page 106)

1 to 2 bird's eye chiles or 1 jalapeño (see Shopsmart, page 106)

1 bunch fresh cilantro or mint

1 lime

1 head red leaf or 2 heads Boston or Bibb or 10-ounce bag prewashed salad greens, preferably an Asian mix (see Shopsmart, page 106)

1 cup mung bean sprouts (optional)

1 large handful roasted peanuts or cashews (about ½ cup)

1. Brush the steak with about ¼ cup of the miso dressing. Marinate at room temperature for up to an hour or cook immediately. When ready to cook, position a broiler pan on the rack closest to the broiler and preheat to high.

2. Carefully lay the steak in the center of the hot pan and broil until the steak is browned but still tender to the touch, about 4 minutes. Turn the steak and broil another 2 to 3 minutes for medium rare (an instant-read thermometer inserted sideways into the steak will register about 130°F). Transfer the steak to a cutting board to rest for 5 to 10 minutes.

3. Thinly slice the white and green parts of the scallions. Peel the carrot. Thinly slice the cucumber, carrot, and chiles. Tear off and discard any tough stems from the cilantro; wash and dry the leaves. Cut the lime into thin wedges.

4. Wash and dry the lettuce. Arrange on a large platter or individual serving plates, along with the vegetables, sprouts, if using, nuts, chiles, and cilantro. Thinly slice the steak against the grain and add to the platter. Garnish with the lime wedges. Serve, passing the remaining dressing at the table.

Editor's Note

While this recipe calls for either cilantro or mint, a combination of both herbs (half a bunch of each) makes the salad especially fragrant and refreshing.

MAKE IT YOUR OWN

Serve this with big lettuce leaves and extra dressing alongside and have your guests make their own lettuce wraps.

SHOPSMART

Asian-labeled mixed greens tend to have tangy, sharp add-ins like mizuna and tatsoi, which add mustardy zip to salads. If you can't find them, look for baby spinach or arugula.

Kirby cucumbers are small and thin-skinned (they look like fresh pickles).

Bird's eye chiles, sometimes called piri-piri, are small, fiery chiles sold both fresh and dried.

Sriracha-Miso Dressing

MAKES ABOUT 1 CUP • PREP TIME: 5 MINUTES

- 1 1-inch piece fresh ginger
- 3 tablespoons yellow (shiro) miso
- 2 tablespoons water
- 1 tablespoon rice vinegar (not the seasoned kind)
- 1 teaspoon soy sauce
- ½ teaspoon Asian chile paste, such as Sriracha or sambal oelek
- ½ cup peanut oil

EQUIPMENT: BLENDER

Peel the ginger. Drop the ginger into the blender and process until finely chopped. Add the miso, water, vinegar, soy sauce, and chile paste; puree. With the blender running, drizzle in the peanut oil to make a smooth, slightly thick dressing. Serve or refrigerate in a tightly sealed container for up to 3 days.

best of the best exclusive

Sweet-and-Sour Catfish

4 SERVINGS

  3 tablespoons fresh lime juice (from 1 lime), plus lime wedges, for serving

  3 tablespoons Asian fish sauce

  3 tablespoons sugar

  2 tablespoons peanut oil

  6 scallions—white and light green parts finely chopped, dark green parts cut into 1-inch lengths

  3 tablespoons minced fresh ginger

  1 stalk of fresh lemongrass, tender white inner bulb only, minced

Four 5-ounce skinless catfish or salmon fillets (about 1¼ pounds), halved lengthwise

Freshly ground pepper

  ¾ cup grape tomatoes, halved lengthwise

  ½ cup mixed fresh basil, mint and cilantro leaves, coarsely chopped

1. In a small bowl, stir the lime juice with the fish sauce and sugar. In a very large skillet, heat the peanut oil. Add the finely chopped scallions, ginger and lemongrass and cook over moderately high heat until fragrant, about 1 minute. Push the ingredients to one side of the skillet.

2. Season the catfish with pepper. Add the fillets to the skillet and cook until lightly golden, about 3 minutes. Turn the fish. Stir in the lime juice mixture, scallion greens and the ingredients at the side of the skillet. Cook until the sauce has thickened and the catfish fillets are white throughout, about 2 minutes. Transfer the fish to a platter and pour the sauce on top. Scatter the tomatoes and chopped herbs over the fish and serve with lime wedges.

Editor's Note

Food Network Kitchens didn't have space to include this wonderfully fresh, bright-flavored fish dish in *How to Boil Water*. We love the sweet and tangy sauce, which would suit any bold-flavored fish, like trout or bluefish.

Mexican Chicken Soup, p. 110

Barefoot Contessa at Home

By Ina Garten

"I find cooking stressful, so anything I can do to take the stress out of it is good," says Food Network personality Ina Garten on the inspiration behind her fifth cookbook, a collection of streamlined recipes for homey-yet-sophisticated favorites like Mexican Chicken Soup, Grilled Tuna Salad and Cornish Hens with Cornbread Stuffing. Filled with helpful tips, easy-to-find ingredients and page after page of unbelievably delicious-looking pictures, this inspiring and user-friendly book can motivate just about anyone to get cooking.

Published by Clarkson Potter, $35.
Find more recipes by Ina Garten at foodandwine.com/garten

Mexican Chicken Soup

Editor's Note

Garten roasts chicken breasts for this soup, but any cooked chicken meat—light or dark—can be used. For a spicier soup, leave the seeds in some of the jalapeños.

As much as I love Mexican food, I always hesitate to order it in restaurants because of my aversion to cilantro. So many people have raved about Mexican chicken soup, though, that I decided to try making it at home. It's really delicious—and, of course, you can always add cilantro.

SERVES 6 TO 8

4 split (2 whole) chicken breasts, bone in, skin on

Good olive oil

Kosher salt and freshly ground black pepper

2 cups chopped yellow onions (2 onions)

1 cup chopped celery (2 stalks)

2 cups chopped carrots (4 carrots)

4 large garlic cloves, chopped

2½ quarts chicken stock, preferably homemade

1 (28-ounce) can whole tomatoes in purée, crushed (see Notes)

2 to 4 jalapeño peppers, seeded and minced (see Notes)

1 teaspoon ground cumin

1 teaspoon ground coriander seed

¼ to ½ cup chopped fresh cilantro (optional)

6 (6-inch) fresh white corn tortillas

TO SERVE

Sliced avocado

Sour cream

Grated Cheddar cheese

Tortilla chips (see Notes)

Preheat the oven to 350 degrees. Place the chicken breasts skin side up on a sheet pan. Rub with olive oil, sprinkle with salt and pepper, and roast for 35 to 40 minutes, until done. When the chicken is cool enough to handle, discard the skin and bones, and shred the meat. Cover and set aside.

Meanwhile, heat 3 tablespoons of olive oil in a large pot or Dutch oven. Add the onions, celery, and carrots and cook over medium-low heat for 10 minutes, or until the onions start to brown. Add the garlic and cook for 30 seconds. Add the chicken stock, tomatoes with their purée, jalapeños, cumin, coriander, 1 tablespoon salt (depending on the saltiness of the chicken stock), 1 teaspoon pepper, and the cilantro, if using. Cut the tortillas in half, then cut them crosswise into ½-inch strips and add to the soup. Bring the soup to a boil, then lower the heat and simmer for 25 minutes. Add the shredded chicken and season to taste. Serve the soup hot topped with sliced avocado, a dollop of sour cream, grated Cheddar cheese, and broken tortilla chips.

NOTES

To crush whole tomatoes, you can either crush them with your hand or pulse them a few times in the bowl of a food processor fitted with a steel blade.

Be very careful handling jalapeños! Cut them in half, scrape out the seeds, and cut them into a small dice. Wash your hands after working with the peppers.

If you want to make your own tortilla chips for garnish, cut 3 corn tortillas in strips and fry in olive oil over medium heat until golden brown. Drain on paper towels.

Grilled Tuna Salad

Editor's Note

Toasting sesame seeds deepens their flavor. Place the seeds in a dry sauté pan and cook over low heat for 5 to 10 minutes, tossing often, until they turn a golden brown. Remove from the pan immediately.

SERVES 4 TO 5

2 pounds very fresh tuna steak, 1-inch thick

Good olive oil

Kosher salt and freshly ground black pepper

Grated zest of 2 limes

6 tablespoons freshly squeezed lime juice (3 limes)

1 teaspoon wasabi powder

2 teaspoons soy sauce

10 dashes Tabasco sauce

2 firm, ripe Hass avocados, large-diced (see Note)

½ red onion, thinly sliced

¼ cup minced scallions, white and green parts (2 scallions)

1 to 2 tablespoons toasted sesame seeds

Heat a charcoal grill with hot coals. Brush the grill with oil.

Brush both sides of the tuna with olive oil and sprinkle generously with salt and pepper. Cook the tuna over the hot coals for about 2½ minutes on each side. Remove to a plate. The tuna should be seared on the outside and raw inside. Allow to cool slightly and cut into large bite-size cubes.

(If you don't want to heat a grill, you can sear the tuna in a dry sauté pan over high heat. Heat the pan for 2 minutes, add the tuna steaks, and cook for 2 to 3 minutes on each side, until seared on the outside and still raw inside.)

For the dressing, whisk together ¼ cup of olive oil, the lime zest and juice, wasabi, soy sauce, Tabasco, 2½ teaspoons salt, and ½ teaspoon pepper.

Toss the avocados in the dressing and then arrange the avocados, tuna, and red onion on individual plates. Drizzle with more dressing and sprinkle with scallions and toasted sesame seeds. Serve at room temperature.

NOTE To prepare the avocados, cut them in half, remove the seed, and ease the flesh out of the rind. Place on a board and dice them. Coat immediately with extra lime juice or vinaigrette to keep them from turning brown.

Cornish Hens with Cornbread Stuffing

Garten on Cornish Hens

I like to shake up tradition on Thanksgiving by giving everyone their own little bird. In the stuffing, you'll want to use corn bread that's moist and not too sweet. These are also easy to make for a dinner party.

SERVES 6

FOR THE STUFFING

- ¼ pound (1 stick) unsalted butter
- 1 cup chopped yellow onion
- 1½ cups medium-diced celery (3 stalks)
- 3 tablespoons chopped fresh flat-leaf parsley
- 5 cups (13 ounces) coarsely crumbled cornbread
- ½ cup chicken stock, preferably homemade

FOR THE HENS

- 6 fresh Cornish hens (1¼- to 1½-pounds)
- 2 cups sliced yellow onions (2 onions)
- Kosher salt and freshly ground black pepper
- 2 tablespoons unsalted butter, melted

Preheat the oven to 400 degrees.

For the stuffing, melt the butter in a medium sauté pan, add the onion, and cook over medium-low heat for 8 minutes, until translucent. Off the heat, add the celery, parsley, cornbread, and chicken stock and mix well. Set aside.

For the hens, rinse them inside and out, removing any pin feathers, and pat the outsides dry. In a roasting pan that's just large enough to hold the hens loosely, first toss in the onions and then place the hens on top, breast side up. Sprinkle the insides of the hens with salt and pepper and loosely fill the cavities with the stuffing. (If there is stuffing left over, bake it in a separate pan until heated through.) Tie the legs of each hen together and tuck the wings under the bodies. Brush with melted butter, sprinkle with salt and pepper, and roast for 50 to 60 minutes, until the skin is browned and the juices run clear when you cut between a leg and thigh. Remove from the oven, cover with aluminum foil, and allow to rest for 15 minutes. Serve a whole hen per person.

Pastel homes line the steep
hillsides of the Ligurian coast.

A Ligurian Kitchen

By Laura Giannatempo

After spending her childhood summers in Liguria, on the Italian Riviera, New York–based food writer Laura Giannatempo developed a passion for the area, with its abundance of seafood and vegetables. Her book is a mix of traditional recipes, such as Soft Chickpea Flatbread with Onions and Thyme, and personal dishes inspired by the region, like Ligurian Ratatouille with Black Olives and Toasted Pine Nuts. A glossary of Italian terms, such as *preboggion* (a Ligurian mix of wild herbs), helps readers navigate the book with ease.

Published by Hippocrene Books, $29.

Pan-Steamed Swordfish with Capers, Olives, and Toasted Pine Nuts

Pesce Spada con Capperi, Olive, e Pinoli

Giannatempo on Vermentino

Like most Ligurian wines, Vermentino goes perfectly with the area's fish and seafood. I use it to give this dish a Ligurian character, but any light, balanced wine with mineral, grassy qualities is fine— an unoaked Sauvignon Blanc is a good substitute.

This dish is similar to *Pesce Spada alla Stimpirata*, which is really a traditional Sicilian dish. But I added a few Ligurian "touches" for this book. I love it: It's a quick and satisfying dish that you, too, will want to have in your repertoire. I make it often, in Liguria as well as in New York.

SERVES 4

¼ cup pine nuts

4 swordfish steaks (about ½ pound each)

Salt

Freshly ground black pepper

4 tablespoons extra-virgin olive oil

½ large onion or 1 small onion, thinly sliced

1 cup coarsely chopped olives (black and green)

1 tablespoon salted capers, rinsed

½ cup Vermentino white wine

¼ cup homemade fish broth (recipe follows) or water

Toast the pine nuts in an 8-inch skillet over medium-high heat until they turn slightly tan, about 4 to 5 minutes. Remove them from the heat and transfer them to a cold plate. This will stop the cooking.

Season the swordfish generously with salt and pepper.

Heat 3 tablespoons of the olive oil in a 12- to 14-inch nonstick skillet (or two 10-inch skillets) over medium-high heat. When the oil is hot, add the fish and sear it over medium-high heat for 3 to 5 minutes on each side. Transfer to a plate near the stove.

Add the remaining oil and the onions to the pan and cook over medium-high heat, stirring frequently, for about 7 to 8 minutes, until the onions are soft and start turning brown on the edges. Add the olives and capers, and cook for another 2 to 3 minutes. Add half of the wine and scrape the bottom of the pan with a wooden spoon. Let the wine completely evaporate. Add the fish back to the pan and pour in the rest of the wine and the broth (or water).

Turn down the heat to medium and cook, partially covered, for 5 to 8 minutes, or until the fish is cooked through but not overdone. Remove from the heat, adjust seasoning with salt and pepper, and sprinkle the pine nuts over the fish. Serve immediately, making sure to spoon some onions, olives, and capers with each serving.

Homemade Fish Broth

MAKES ABOUT 1 GALLON (16 CUPS) BROTH

8 to 10 pounds fish bones and trimmings

8 ounces onion (about 1 large onion), quartered

4 ounces celery (about 2 medium stalks), cut into 2-inch pieces

4 ounces carrots (about 1 large carrot), cut into 2-inch pieces

1 bay leaf

5 sprigs parsley

2 sprigs thyme

10 black peppercorns

16 cups cold water

1 cup dry white wine (optional)

Combine the fish bones, onions, celery, carrot, bay leaf, parsley, thyme, and peppercorns in a large stockpot. Add the water, plus the wine, if using, and bring to a boil. Reduce to a slow simmer and simmer, uncovered, for 50 to 60 minutes.

Strain the broth through a fine-mesh strainer into a large bowl. Place the bowl in an ice bath and let it cool, covered with plastic wrap, before you refrigerate or freeze it. I like to freeze broth in 1-pint containers so when I need only a little bit, I don't have to defrost an entire quart.

Soft Chickpea Flatbread with Onions and Thyme

Farinata con Cipolle e Timo

Giannatempo on Chickpea Flour

Farinata is a pancake-like chickpea-flour flatbread that is traditionally served in Liguria as a snack, but also makes a nice appetizer. Chickpea or garbanzo flour—also called *farina di ceci*—is available at natural food stores and Italian specialty markets. Indian chickpea flour, which is made from a different legume, shouldn't be substituted.

SERVES 4 TO 6

- 2 cups (½ pound) chickpea flour
- 3 cups water
- 1 tablespoon plus ½ teaspoon salt, plus more for seasoning the onions
- ½ cup plus 3 tablespoons extra-virgin olive oil
- 2 small sweet onions, thinly sliced
- 2 tablespoons chopped thyme

Freshly ground black pepper

Place the chickpea flour in a large bowl and slowly add the water, whisking constantly to prevent clumps. You'll end up with a fairly liquid batter.

Add the salt, stir, and let the batter rest, covered with plastic wrap, for at least four hours at room temperature.

In a 12-inch skillet, heat 3 tablespoons of the olive oil over medium-high heat. When the oil is hot, add the onions. Add a small pinch of salt and cook, stirring frequently, over medium-high heat for about 8 minutes, allowing the onions to brown a little without burning. Add 1 or 2 tablespoons of water if the onions start sticking to the pan or become too dark. Turn down the heat to medium and continue cooking the onions for another 15 minutes, stirring frequently and adding a few tablespoons of warm water as the onions begin to dry. At the end, the onions should be a light brown color and glossy. Set them aside.

Preheat the oven to 425°F.

With a large slotted spoon, remove any foam that might have formed on the surface of the batter, and stir the batter well. Pour the remaining olive oil in a 17 x 13-inch rimmed baking sheet (preferably nonstick) and pour in the batter. Spread it with the back of a wooden spoon to cover the pan and to incorporate the oil. The batter should form only a thin layer, about ¼ inch thick.

Top the batter with the onions and thyme, distributing them evenly.

Bake for 35 to 40 minutes or until golden brown. Let it rest for a few minutes and sprinkle on some pepper. Use a pizza cutter to slice, and serve warm.

Ligurian Ratatouille with Black Olives and Toasted Pine Nuts
Ratatuia

This is the Ligurian cousin of the popular southern French dish. You'll find it uses a greater variety of vegetables than French ratatouille with a sprinkle of the ubiquitous toasted pine nuts. You can choose to serve it warm or at room temperature, but I find it tastes better if it sits a few hours before you reheat it and serve.

SERVES 4

- 3 ounces green beans, cut into 1-inch pieces (about ¾ cup)
- 3 medium-size yellow, red, and/or orange bell peppers
- ⅓ cup plus 3 tablespoons good extra-virgin olive oil
- 2 small zucchini, cut into ½-inch dice (about 1⅓ cups)
- 1 small yellow squash, cut into ½-inch dice (about ⅔ cup)

Salt

- 1 small onion, finely chopped (about 1 tightly packed cup)
- 1 large clove garlic, finely chopped (about 1½ teaspoons)
- 1 medium eggplant or 3 baby eggplants, cut into ½-inch dice (about 2 cups)
- 1 large carrot, cut into ⅛ x 1-inch strips
- 3 plum tomatoes, peeled, seeded, and coarsely chopped
- ½ cup pitted black olives, preferably a mixture of gaeta, niçoise, and oil-cured
- 8 basil leaves, torn roughly by hand

Freshly ground black pepper

- 1 tablespoon toasted pine nuts

Preheat the oven to 450°F.

Bring a large pot of water to a boil and add the green beans. Cook them for about 5 minutes (they should be tender but still quite al dente). Drain, and shock them under cold running water or in a bowl of ice water. Drain them again.

Giannatempo on Ratatouille

I think it's important to sauté ingredients with different cooking times and textures separately so they retain their distinctive flavors. Then I heat them all in the pan with a little tomato to help bring them together.

Ligurian Ratatouille with Black Olives and Toasted Pine Nuts

Place the peppers on a baking sheet lined with aluminum foil and roast for 30 to 40 minutes, or until soft and slightly charred on the outside. Place them in a bowl, cover it with plastic wrap, let rest for about 10 minutes, then remove the skins. Cut the peppers into ½-inch-wide strips.

In a 10-inch skillet, heat 1 tablespoon of the olive oil over medium-high heat. When the oil is hot, add the zucchini, yellow squash, and a pinch of salt, and cook, stirring frequently, for 5 to 7 minutes, or until the vegetables are soft and slightly browned. Set aside.

In a 12-inch skillet, heat ⅓ cup of the olive oil over medium-high heat. When the oil is hot, add the onion and garlic, and cook for 3 to 4 minutes, stirring frequently (be careful not to burn the garlic). Add the eggplant, carrots, and a small pinch of salt, and cook for about 5 more minutes. Add the tomatoes, olives, four of the basil leaves, and another small pinch of salt, and cook for another 10 to 15 minutes, stirring frequently and adding a few tablespoons of warm water if the ingredients in the pan seem to be too dry (but allow the veggies to brown a little and stick to the pan before adding water). By now the vegetables in the pan should be fairly tender.

Add the sautéed zucchini and squash, the roasted peppers, the blanched green beans, and the remaining basil leaves to the pan and cook for 3 to 5 minutes. Adjust the seasoning with salt, add a few generous grinds of pepper, the pine nuts, and finish with the remaining 2 tablespoons of olive oil. Don't hesitate to add more olive oil if the *ratatuia* looks dry.

best of the best exclusive

Risotto with Sweet Sausage and Fennel

Editor's Note

If you want to add a touch of citrus flavor to this risotto, stir in ¼ teaspoon finely grated orange zest along with the butter, Parmesan cheese and parsley.

6 SERVINGS

- ¼ cup plus 1 teaspoon extra-virgin olive oil
- 1 large fennel bulb—halved, cored and thinly sliced crosswise
- 2 teaspoons minced garlic
- ½ pound sweet Italian sausage, casings removed
- 5¼ cups chicken stock or low-sodium broth
- 4 tablespoons unsalted butter
- 1 medium onion, finely chopped
- 1 medium leek, white and light green parts only, finely chopped
- 1 celery rib, finely chopped

Kosher salt

- 2 cups arborio rice (14 ounces)
- 1 cup dry white wine
- 1 cup freshly grated Parmigiano-Reggiano cheese, plus more for serving
- 1 tablespoon coarsely chopped flat-leaf parsley

Freshly ground black pepper

1. In a large skillet, heat 2 tablespoons of the olive oil. Add the fennel and ½ teaspoon of the garlic and cook over moderately high heat until the fennel is tender and beginning to brown, about 8 minutes. Transfer the fennel to a plate and wipe out the skillet.

2. Heat 1 teaspoon of the olive oil in the skillet. Add the sausage and cook over moderately high heat, breaking it up with the back of a spoon, until cooked through and browned, about 4 minutes. Add the sausage to the fennel.

3. In a saucepan, bring the stock to a simmer; cover and keep hot. In a very large, deep skillet, melt 1 tablespoon of the butter in the remaining 2 tablespoons of olive oil. Add the onion, leek, celery, the remaining 1½ teaspoons of garlic and a pinch of salt. Cook over moderate heat until the onion is softened, about 5 minutes. Add the rice and cook, stirring, for 1 minute. Add the wine and cook, stirring, until almost absorbed, about 2 minutes. Gradually add the hot stock, ½ cup at a time, stirring constantly until all of the stock has been absorbed before adding more, about 18 minutes total. The risotto is done when the rice is just tender and the sauce is creamy. Stir in the fennel and sausage and cook for 1 minute. Remove from the heat and stir in the remaining 3 tablespoons of butter, the 1 cup of Parmigiano-Reggiano and the parsley. Season with salt and pepper and serve, passing additional cheese at the table.

Linguine with Frenched Green Beans
and Parsley "Pesto," p. 128

On Top of Spaghetti...

By Johanne Killeen & George Germon

If only every chef could create perfect recipes for the home cook as deftly as Johanne Killeen and George Germon. Owners of Al Forno in Providence, the couple has been serving some of the best Italian-influenced food in the country for over 25 years. In this cookbook, Killeen says, "We wanted to explore different ways of looking at pasta—to use the Italian model, but with indigenous, American ingredients." Using pantry staples like tomato paste and walnuts, they create wonderful dishes of unexpected complexity.

Published by William Morrow, $24.95.
Find more recipes by Killeen and Germon at foodandwine.com/killeen-germon

Linguine with Frenched Green Beans and Parsley "Pesto"

Frenching green beans fell out of fashion years ago, which is too bad because the technique is worth a comeback. Thinly sliced, slivered beans have a different, more appealing texture and taste. It is worthwhile finding the gadget (a closely spaced series of three or four blades through which the bean passes, resulting in julienne slices) that makes easy work of the cutting process. A good, sharp knife will also do the trick. If using a knife, cut the beans into as many vertical, thin slices as you can manage (the finer the slivers, the better they will twirl around your fork with the linguine). Take your time and tuck in your fingertips to avoid nicking them with the knife blade.

This spirited emerald green-on-green pasta sauce has a fresh flavor. The parsley and basil wake up the taste of the beans without overwhelming them. A hint of garlic and just a touch of hot pepper make all the components come alive.

SERVES 6 AS A FIRST COURSE

- 8 ounces fresh green beans, trimmed and sliced lengthwise into thin slivers
- 2 cups gently packed fresh flat-leaf parsley leaves
- 10 large fresh basil leaves
- 1 small garlic clove, trimmed and peeled
- ½ cup light-flavored extra-virgin olive oil
- ½ teaspoon sea salt

Pinch or more of cayenne

- ½ cup freshly grated Pecorino Romano, plus more to pass at the table
- 8 ounces dried linguine

1. Cook the green beans in boiling salted water until tender. They should yield easily under the pressure of your teeth. Drain in a colander and set aside next to the sink to await the pasta.

2. Bring a large pot of water to a boil for the pasta.

3. Whirl the parsley, basil, garlic, olive oil, salt, and cayenne in a blender until you have a chunky purée. Pour into a warmed, but not hot, serving bowl. Stir in ½ cup Pecorino Romano.

4. Generously salt the pasta water and drop in the linguine. Cook, stirring often, until al dente. Reserve about 1 cup of the cooking water, then pour the remaining water and pasta into the colander over the beans. This will warm the beans if they have cooled. Transfer the pasta and beans to the serving bowl and toss with the sauce and cheese. Add enough reserved cooking water, a tablespoon at a time, to loosen the pesto. There should be a small puddle of sauce on the bottom of the bowl. Serve right away with extra Pecorino Romano passed at the table.

Killeen and Germon on Pasta Water

People in this country are getting accustomed to reserving pasta cooking water: If a sauce is too thin, add a little of the starchy water and boil until the sauce has thickened. On the flip side, if a sauce is too thick, add pasta water to thin it.

Shells Baked with Spinach, Herbs, and Walnuts

The flavors of *pansoti con salsa di noci*—herb-and-cheese-filled ravioli with walnut sauce—inspire this unusual baked macaroni. A specialty of Liguria, the *pansoti* are traditionally made with two ingredients that never travel beyond the region—*preboggion*, an intensely flavored herb and plant mixture, and *prescinsena*, a slightly tart cow's milk cheese. A combination of spinach, arugula, and cultivated herbs replaces the indigenous *preboggion*, and the *prescinsena* is replaced with sour cream.

SERVES 6 TO 8 AS A FIRST COURSE OR 4 TO 6 AS A MAIN COURSE

1¼ cups finely chopped onions

  2 fresh bay leaves or 1 dried bay leaf

  1 small garlic clove, peeled and finely minced

  2 tablespoons unsalted butter

  2 tablespoons extra-virgin olive oil

  ½ teaspoon sea salt

2½ cups heavy cream

  4 cups tightly packed baby spinach, borage, watercress, or chicory leaves

  1 cup tightly packed baby arugula leaves

  1 teaspoon finely chopped fresh sage

  ½ teaspoon finely chopped fresh basil

  1 teaspoon finely chopped fresh marjoram

  ¼ teaspoon finely chopped fresh summer savory

  2 teaspoons finely chopped chives

  1 cup finely chopped walnuts

  ½ cup cubed fontina

  ½ cup freshly grated Pecorino Romano

  1 cup freshly grated Parmigiano-Reggiano

Freshly grated nutmeg

  3 tablespoons sour cream or crème fraîche

  1 pound dried *conchiglie rigate,* or ridged pasta shells

1. Combine the onions, bay leaves, garlic, butter, olive oil, and salt in a small saucepan. Sauté over moderately low heat until the onions and garlic are very soft and completely cooked through, about 15 minutes. Add the cream and scald—heat just until little bubbles form around the outside edge. Set aside off the heat for 30 minutes to steep together.

2. Bring a large pot of water to a boil for the pasta. Heat the oven to 500 degrees.

3. In another saucepan, drop the spinach and arugula leaves in boiling salted water. Cook, stirring often, until the greens are wilted, about 2 minutes. Drain in a colander.

4. When the greens are cool enough to handle, squeeze out as much water as possible. Transfer to a cutting board and finely chop. Combine the chopped greens, sage, basil, marjoram, summer savory, and chives in a large mixing bowl. Add the walnuts, fontina, Pecorino Romano, Parmigiano-Reggiano, and a good scraping of nutmeg (a microplane is the ideal tool for this). Remove and discard the bay leaves and add the cooled cream and sour cream to the mixing bowl. Stir to combine. Taste and add salt if necessary. Set aside.

5. Generously salt the boiling water and drop in the pasta. Cook, stirring often, to parboil, 4 to 5 minutes (the pasta will be too hard to eat; it will continue to cook in the oven). Drain the shells, reserving about 1 cup of the water. Toss the pasta with the ingredients in the mixing bowl until well combined; you want the shells to capture some of the walnuts, herbs, and cheese in their crannies. Add ½ cup reserved pasta water and toss again. Transfer to individual shallow baking dishes or a large shallow gratin dish. There should be ample liquid surrounding the pasta. If not, nap with additional pasta water. Bake until bubbly and hot, with some of the pasta shells browning on top. Serve right away.

Killeen and Germon on Variations

The number of greens and herbs in this recipe gives it a complex flavor, but the dish will still taste great even if you can't get them all. The arugula and spinach combo is delicious, but you can also substitute 5 cups of watercress. And if you don't have all the herbs, use 2 or 3—just make sure to include one of the sweet herbs (basil, marjoram or summer savory) and the chives.

Mostaccioli with Tomato "Pesto"

Editor's Note

An uncooked sauce based on ¾ cup tomato paste may sound like it will taste harsh. But blended with pine nuts and olive oil, this richly flavored, simple pesto becomes far more than a sum of its parts.

George developed this recipe for the Al Forno menu. The luxurious texture of pine nuts makes the pesto look creamier than it really is.

When we decided to include the pesto in this book, George handed me a slip of paper with the measurements of ingredients written in "tomato paste cans" instead of cups. While it works perfectly well his way, here is the translation in standard measures.

SERVES 6 TO 8 AS A FIRST COURSE OR 4 TO 6 AS A MAIN COURSE

¾ cup (one 6-ounce can) tomato paste, preferably organic

¾ cup plus 2 tablespoons extra-virgin olive oil

½ cup plus 1 tablespoon pine nuts

¼ teaspoon sea salt

¼ to ½ teaspoon cayenne or crushed red pepper flakes

2 tablespoons tomato juice, preferably organic

2 plump garlic cloves, trimmed, peeled, and roughly chopped

1 pound dried mostaccioli, penne, or rigatoni

Freshly grated Pecorino Romano

1. Bring a large pot of water to a boil.

2. Combine the tomato paste, olive oil, pine nuts, salt, cayenne, tomato juice, and garlic in the bowl of a food processor. Run the motor until you have a smooth purée. Set aside at room temperature while you cook the pasta. (You can cover and refrigerate the pesto, but be sure to bring it to room temperature before boiling the pasta.)

3. Generously salt the boiling water and drop in the mostaccioli. Cook, stirring often, until al dente. Drain, reserving about ½ cup of the pasta water. Transfer the mostaccioli to a heated serving bowl. Add enough of the pesto to coat the noodles generously. Add a little pasta water, a tablespoon at a time, if it seems too thick. Sprinkle with cheese and pass more Pecorino Romano and any remaining pesto at the table.

Spaghetti with Fresh Spinach and Gorgonzola

Killeen and Germon on Ingredients

We seek out tender spinach, which seems less likely to make your teeth feel like they're wearing cashmere sweaters. In the spring you can get young spinach, and during the rest of the year you can use bagged baby spinach leaves. As for the blue cheese, either regular or *dolce* (sweet) Gorgonzola will work here: The important thing is to choose one you love to eat.

In early spring, look for tender spinach with small leaves at the local farmers' market. It is so flavorful that it needs nothing more than a bit of Gorgonzola and butter to make a memorable dish.

SERVES 6 TO 8 AS A FIRST COURSE OR 4 TO 6 AS A MAIN COURSE

- 4 ounces Gorgonzola, at room temperature
- 4 tablespoons unsalted butter, at room temperature
- 8 cups firmly packed trimmed young, fresh spinach
- 2 tablespoons extra-virgin olive oil
- 2 teaspoons sea salt
- 1 pound dried spaghetti or spaghettini

10 to 12 large fresh basil leaves (optional)

1. Bring a large pot of water to a boil for the pasta.

2. In a small bowl, mush together the Gorgonzola and butter until you have a smooth paste. Set aside but do not refrigerate.

3. Wash the spinach in plenty of cold water. Drain in a colander, leaving the water clinging to the leaves.

4. Heat the olive oil in a large straight-sided skillet over moderately high heat. Add the spinach and 1 teaspoon of the salt. Toss the spinach with tongs until it has wilted. Taste it and add more salt if necessary. Turn off the heat, but keep the spinach warm on the side of the stove.

5. Generously salt the pasta water and drop in the spaghetti. Cook at a rolling boil, stirring often, until al dente. Drain the pasta, reserving about 1 cup of the cooking water. Transfer the spaghetti to the skillet and toss with the spinach. Add the Gorgonzola-butter mixture and toss to coat each strand of spaghetti. If the pasta seems dry, add a bit of cooking water and toss again. Add as much of the cooking water as you need to make a creamy consistency. If you have fresh basil, tear the leaves and toss into the spaghetti. Serve right away.

best of the best exclusive

Farfalle with Yogurt and Zucchini

Editor's Note
Yogurt is an unexpected ingredient in a pasta dish, and mixing it with butter creates a tangy, creamy sauce that coaxes incredible flavor from a few simple ingredients.

4 TO 6 SERVINGS

- 1 pound farfalle
- 4 medium zucchini (about 1½ pounds), coarsely shredded
- 4 tablespoons unsalted butter
- 1 cup plain whole-milk Greek yogurt
- 1 cup freshly grated Parmigiano-Reggiano cheese, plus more for serving

Freshly grated nutmeg

Kosher salt and freshly ground pepper

1. In a large pot of boiling salted water, cook the farfalle until al dente; about 1 minute before the farfalle is done, add the shredded zucchini to the pot. Drain, reserving ¼ cup of the pasta cooking water.

2. Meanwhile, in a large, deep skillet, melt the butter. Remove from the heat. Stir in the yogurt and the 1 cup of grated Parmigiano-Reggiano and season with nutmeg, salt and pepper.

3. Add the farfalle, zucchini and reserved pasta cooking water to the saucepan and cook over low heat, tossing, until the sauce coats the pasta. Transfer to warmed bowls and serve, passing extra cheese at the table.

Fillet of Sole Piccata
Sandwiches, p. 138

Stonewall Kitchen Favorites

By Jonathan King, Jim Stott & Kathy Gunst

Jonathan King and Jim Stott, the owners of the Maine-based specialty food company Stonewall Kitchen, teamed up with cook and writer Kathy Gunst for their second cookbook, which riffs on traditional American favorites from their childhoods like chicken noodle soup and mac and cheese. They might lighten a recipe by baking instead of frying, or they might modernize it with ingredients like fresh herbs, as in Three Moms' Meat Loaf, which combines all their family recipes— "A mum's a mum, they all make meat loaf," King says.

Published by Clarkson Potter, $32.50.
Find more recipes by the Stonewall team at foodandwine.com/stonewall

Fillet of Sole Piccata Sandwiches

Editor's Note
Caperberries are the berry of the caper bush, and are larger and milder than capers, the immature buds. They come pickled in jars and can be found at specialty food stores.

Piccata refers to a classic Italian dish, usually made with veal or chicken, sautéed in a hot pan and deglazed with lemon, wine, and sometimes capers. Here we use this technique to make one of the most satisfying sandwiches we know of—fillet of sole sautéed with thin slices of lemon, piled onto slices of lightly toasted baguette, and topped with a caperberry-lemon mayonnaise.

Make the mayonnaise ahead of time and the sandwiches can be put together in about 10 minutes!

SERVES 2 TO 4

FOR THE CAPERBERRY-LEMON MAYONNAISE

¼ cup plus 2 tablespoons mayonnaise

¼ cup plus 2 tablespoons thinly sliced caperberries

⅛ cup fresh lemon juice

Freshly ground black pepper

FOR THE SANDWICHES

Two to four 5-inch-long pieces baguette

½ cup all-purpose flour

Salt and freshly ground black pepper

8 ounces fillet of sole

2 tablespoons unsalted butter

2 teaspoons olive oil

1 lemon, preferably organic, washed and cut into paper-thin slices

To make the mayonnaise: In a small bowl, mix the mayonnaise, caperberries, lemon juice, and pepper until smooth. Cover and refrigerate until ready to serve or for up to 2 days.

Cut each piece of baguette in half lengthwise and lightly toast in the toaster or under a broiler.

Place the flour on a plate and season liberally with salt and pepper. Lightly dredge the fish fillets in the seasoned flour.

In a large, heavy skillet set over high heat, add half of the butter and half of the oil and let it get hot. Add half of the fish fillets, being careful not to crowd the pan, and cook for 2 minutes. Gently flip the fish over, add half of the lemon slices to the pan and cook another 2 minutes, or until the fish is golden brown and cooked through. Repeat with the remaining butter, oil, fish, and lemon slices.

Place a baguette half on a plate, and spread about 1 tablespoon of the mayonnaise on top. Place a hot fish fillet and a few of the sautéed lemon slices on top of each half. Top with a dollop of mayonnaise and serve open-faced, or topped with another slice of baguette.

FAVORITE VARIATIONS

Use fillet of lemon sole, flounder, haddock, cod, salmon, or any other white fish instead of the sole.

Use a Meyer lemon or lime instead of the regular lemon.

Use coarsely chopped capers instead of caperberries.

Editor's Note
Caperberry-lemon mayonnaise is like a quick, elegant tartar sauce. It's great with steamed crab or shrimp.

Sautéed Shrimp with Garlic, Lime, and Chile Sauce

The Stonewall Team on Serving

We like these spicy, tangy shrimp as an appetizer or as a main course with couscous, pasta or rice. You can also serve the shrimp over 2 cups of baby arugula or mesclun, pouring the warm sauce on the greens to slightly wilt them.

SERVES 4

1 to 2 tablespoons olive oil

2 garlic cloves, thinly sliced

1 pound large shrimp, shelled and deveined

Juice from 2 limes

¼ to 1 teaspoon Chinese chile paste or hot pepper sauce

½ cup Vermouth or dry white wine

1 lime, cut into wedges for garnish

In a large skillet, heat 1 tablespoon of the oil over medium-high heat. Add the garlic and, stirring, cook for 1 minute. Add the shrimp, in one layer if possible, and cook for 2 minutes. Using tongs, flip the shrimp over and cook for 1 minute.

Add the lime juice and chile paste to taste (¼ teaspoon will provide a hint of spice and 1 teaspoon will sock-it-to-ya!). Raise the heat to high and add the Vermouth. Cook for 1 minute. Remove the shrimp to a platter.

Add the remaining tablespoon oil if you like and boil the juices down in the pan over high heat for another minute. Pour the sauce on top of the shrimp and garnish with the limes.

FAVORITE VARIATIONS

Add any or all along with the garlic:

Roasted or steamed asparagus, cut on the diagonal into 1-inch pieces.

2 chopped scallions (white and green parts).

2 tablespoons julienne strips of peeled, fresh ginger.

Very thin strips of red bell pepper.

½ cup chopped peanuts or cashews added during the last minute of cooking, or sprinkled on as a garnish.

Three Moms' Meat Loaf

Each one of us has distinct childhood memories involving meat loaf. We all grew up eating it in one form or another, and each of us had a kind of a love-hate relationship with the dish. But we decided it was time to take a new look at this American classic. This recipe, a sophisticated, much-improved version of what we remember from days past, combines elements from each of our mothers' best meat loaves.

Three Moms' Meat Loaf combines ground beef, pork, and veal, fresh rosemary, thyme, and parsley and is baked free-form on a baking sheet. The meat loaf stays moist and flavorful thanks to a few strips of bacon placed on top and a simple tomato sauce that forms in the pan. If you are lucky enough to have any leftovers, the meat loaf makes a fabulous sandwich the next day.

SERVES 6 TO 8

- 1 tablespoon olive oil
- 1 small onion, chopped
- 2 garlic cloves, minced
- 1 pound ground beef chuck (see Note, page 142)
- 12 ounces ground pork (see Note, page 142)
- 12 ounces ground veal (see Note, page 142)
- 2 large eggs
- 1 cup plain bread crumbs
- 1 tablespoon tomato paste
- ¼ cup chopped fresh parsley leaves
- 2 tablespoons chopped fresh thyme leaves
- 1 tablespoon chopped fresh rosemary leaves
- 2 teaspoons salt

Freshly ground black pepper

One 16-ounce can crushed tomatoes

- 4 ounces thick-sliced bacon (about 4 slices)

King on Variations

You can shape this mixture into mini meat loaves like we do at the Stonewall Kitchen Cafe, or you can form it into meatballs, sauté them, then add them to pasta sauce. If you have leftover meat loaf, you can cut it into cubes, rewarm it in marinara sauce, and toss it with pasta and Parmesan cheese.

Place a rack in the middle of the oven and preheat oven to 375°F.

Heat the olive oil in a medium skillet over medium-low heat. When hot, add the onion and garlic and cook, stirring occasionally, until the onion is soft, about 10 minutes.

In a large bowl, combine the onion mixture, beef, pork, veal, eggs, bread crumbs, tomato paste, parsley, thyme, rosemary, salt, and a generous grinding of pepper, mixing well with your hands or a wooden spoon. Turn the meat out onto a rimmed baking sheet, a roasting pan with high edges, or a large 11 x 15-inch or 9 x 13-inch glass dish and form the meat mixture into a loaf approximately 5 x 8 inches and 3 to 4 inches tall. Mix the tomatoes with 1½ cups water in a small bowl and pour the sauce over the top of the meat loaf, allowing some of it to fall into the pan. Drape the bacon strips over the meat loaf widthwise.

Bake for 30 minutes, basting with the pan juices several times. Increase the oven temperature to 400°F, and bake an additional 30 to 40 minutes, basting every 10 minutes or so, for a total cooking time of 60 to 70 minutes. The bacon should be cooked through and a thermometer inserted into the center of the meat loaf should measure 165°F. Remove from the oven and let the meat loaf rest for 10 minutes, then cut into slices and serve with the bacon and the tomato juices from the bottom of the pan.

NOTE If you can't find all three meats (often found premixed with the label "meat loaf mix" in supermarkets), try a mixture of whatever ground red meats you can find, totaling 2½ pounds. For the best flavor, make sure the meat has at least 10 percent fat (this is generally listed on the label).

FAVORITE VARIATIONS

Add ¾ cup freshly grated Parmesan cheese for a richer meat loaf.

Finely chop 1 small red or green bell pepper and add it to the pan with the onions and garlic.

Substitute fresh basil for the parsley.

Stonewall Kitchen
Favorites
*By Jonathan King,
Jim Stott & Kathy Gunst*

best of the best exclusive

Parmesan Chicken with Baby Arugula Salad

4 SERVINGS

- 4 skinless, boneless chicken breast halves (about 1¾ pounds)
- 1 garlic clove
- 1 cup *panko* (Japanese bread crumbs)
- ½ cup freshly grated Parmesan cheese
- ¼ cup coarsely chopped flat-leaf parsley

Kosher salt and freshly ground pepper

- 2 large eggs
- ½ cup extra-virgin olive oil
- ¼ pound baby arugula
- 1 tablespoon balsamic vinegar

Lemon wedges, for serving

1. On a work surface, arrange the chicken breasts between 2 sheets of plastic wrap. Pound the breasts to a ½-inch thickness.

2. In a food processor, pulse the garlic clove until finely chopped. Add the *panko,* Parmesan and parsley and pulse until the parsley is finely chopped; season with salt and pepper. Transfer the *panko* mixture to a shallow bowl.

3. In another shallow bowl, beat the eggs and season them with salt and pepper. Season the chicken breasts with salt and pepper. Dip the chicken in the egg, letting the excess drip back into the dish, then dredge in the *panko* mixture to coat completely.

4. In a large skillet, heat ¼ cup of the olive oil until shimmering. Add 2 of the chicken breasts and fry, turning once, until golden brown all over, about 7 minutes. Transfer to paper towels to drain. Add 2 tablespoons of the olive oil to the skillet and repeat with the remaining 2 chicken breasts.

5. Meanwhile, in a large bowl, toss the arugula with the remaining 2 tablespoons of olive oil and the balsamic vinegar. Transfer the arugula to plates and top with the chicken breasts. Serve with lemon wedges.

Editor's Note

Jonathan King's recipe for deliciously juicy and crispy chicken cutlets calls for pounding chicken breasts. To eliminate that step, you can buy prepounded cutlets.

Crispy Fried Okra, p. 146

The Lee Bros. Southern Cookbook

By Matt Lee & Ted Lee

"This is our dream version of the definitive Southern cookbook," say Matt Lee and Ted Lee. The brothers moved as children from Manhattan to Charleston, South Carolina. "We didn't grow up with a Southern grandma and our own recipe box. That liberated us to be more creative in the kitchen," Ted says. In addition to excellent recipes—both traditional and updated—the Lees share quirky accounts of Southern food legends and history, as well as plenty of practical advice, including ingredient sources, drink pairings and recipe variations.

Published by W. W. Norton & Company, $35.
Find more recipes by Matt Lee and Ted Lee at foodandwine.com/leebros

Crispy Fried Okra

Editor's Note

The easiest way to coat the okra is to toss it with the wet ingredients, then scoop the pieces out with a slotted spoon, shaking off excess, before tossing them with the dry ingredients.

Fried okra is a dynamite side dish for all sorts of entrées. But it's as addictive as popcorn, so we often pass it during cocktail hour as a snack. Keep the fried okra warm in the oven in an uncovered earthenware dish. When the first guests arrive, fill a few butcher-paper or newspaper cones with the okra, shake some chile flakes and sea salt over them, and pass the cones around while the guests are tucking into their cocktails.

MAKES 2 POUNDS; ENOUGH FOR 6 TO 8 AS A SIDE DISH, AND 12 FOR SNACKING

TIME: 30 MINUTES

- 4 cups peanut or canola oil
- 2 large eggs, beaten
- ¾ cup whole milk
- 2 cups stone-ground cornmeal
- 3 tablespoons all-purpose flour
- 1½ teaspoons salt
- 1½ teaspoons freshly ground black pepper
- 2 pounds fresh okra, sliced into ½-inch-thick rounds (about 7 cups)

Crushed red pepper flakes to taste (optional)

Sea salt to taste (optional)

1. Preheat the oven to 225 degrees. Heat the oil in a 12-inch cast-iron skillet or a 3-quart enameled cast-iron casserole until the temperature on a candy thermometer reads 375 degrees.

2. In a large bowl, whisk together the eggs and milk until they are well combined, about 1 minute. In a medium bowl, sift the cornmeal, flour, salt, and pepper together twice. Add the okra to the egg mixture and toss until it is evenly coated. Scatter half the dredge over the okra and toss to coat. Scatter the remaining dredge over the okra and toss again.

3. Transfer about ⅓ of the okra to the oil with a slotted spoon and fry in batches, turning as necessary with the spoon, until the slices are golden brown all over, about 2 minutes per batch.

4. Using the slotted spoon, transfer the okra to a plate lined with a double thickness of paper towels. When it has drained, transfer to a ceramic serving dish that holds heat well and place in the oven until ready to serve.

5. Dust the okra with red pepper flakes and sea salt, if desired, and pass a cruet of Pepper Vinegar (recipe follows) around the table when you serve.

Pepper Vinegar

We always bring a cruet of pepper vinegar to the table along with the salt and pepper. It's a great hot sauce to shake on everything from a fried oyster to a morsel of pork shoulder. It's also a superb tenderizer for meats and an easy way to gussy up a favorite salad dressing. Best of all, making it is very, very easy. You can use fresh or dried hot peppers, but fresh ones give the vinegar kick for longer. Just keep topping up your cruet with vinegar until the peppers no longer give it heat. You'll be surprised how long-lasting hot peppers are. Some cruets we've had are on their third year, and the vinegar seems as fiery as the first day we made it.

MAKES 2 CUPS
TIME: 2 MINUTES TO PREPARE, 24 HOURS TO CHILL

1 cup white wine vinegar
2 Thai, serrano, or bird's-eye chiles, fresh or dried

With a funnel, pour the vinegar into a cruet. Add the chiles and use a chopstick or the handle of a wooden spoon to submerge them, if necessary. Cap the cruet and place it in the refrigerator. The vinegar will be well infused in 24 hours and will keep for months in the refrigerator.

The Lees on Choosing Okra

Okra grows in the U.S. all summer long, and it's flown to Latin markets here from South America in the winter. Choose bright green pods that are on the smaller side—they will be more tender—and avoid any that are spotted or woody.

Sweet Potato Buttermilk Pie

This is a Lee Bros. original, born of our boredom with conventional sweet potato pies, which we find often to be leaden and dull. (One notable exception is a sweet potato pie we ate at the home of the Texas sweet potato farmers Rona and Dale Smith, which had a fabulous crunchy Rice Krispies, brown sugar, and butter topping.) We wanted our pie to resemble the light, tangy buttermilk pie Robert Stehling of the Hominy Grill makes. So we whisked sweet potato puree into a filling we adapted from Stehling's recipe for buttermilk pie, and the result was astonishing. Some have compared it to a cross between sweet potato pie and cheesecake, which rings true when you taste it. But we'd like to note that it doesn't weigh on you the way cheesecake does. It's ethereal, frothy, and divine, and it just may be our most crowd-pleasing dessert.

FOR 6 PEOPLE

TIME: 1 HOUR, 10 MINUTES

- 1½ pounds sweet potatoes (about 2 medium potatoes), peeled and chopped into ½-inch dice
- 4 tablespoons unsalted butter, melted
- 2 tablespoons fresh lemon juice
- ½ teaspoon freshly grated nutmeg
- ½ teaspoon ground cinnamon
- ½ teaspoon kosher salt
- 3 large eggs, separated
- ½ cup sugar
- 2 tablespoons all-purpose flour
- ¾ cup whole or lowfat buttermilk (preferably whole)
- 1 Sweet Pie Crust (recipe follows), prebaked

1. Preheat the oven to 375 degrees.

2. Pour 1½ inches of water into a 3-quart stockpot with a strainer basket and bring to a boil over medium-high heat. Add the sweet potatoes, cover, and steam until fork-tender, about 20 minutes. Strain the sweet potatoes, place in a large bowl, and let cool to room temperature. Mash them to a smooth puree with a fork or a potato masher. You should have 1¼ cups puree; discard any excess. Add the butter, lemon juice, nutmeg, cinnamon, and salt, mixing thoroughly with a wooden spoon or rubber spatula after each addition.

3. In a small bowl, beat the egg yolks lightly with a whisk, about 30 seconds. Add the sugar and beat until they're a creamy lemon-yellow color, about 1½ minutes. Add the egg mixture to the sweet potato mixture and stir with a wooden spoon or rubber spatula until the eggs are thoroughly incorporated and the filling is a consistent bright orange color. Add the flour a little at a time, stirring after each addition, until thoroughly incorporated. Add the buttermilk and stir to incorporate.

4. Wash the whisk in a stream of hot water to wash away any butter residue, then rinse in cold water to cool it down and dry with a paper towel. In a separate bowl, whisk the egg whites to soft peaks, about 1½ minutes. With a wooden spoon or rubber spatula, gently fold the egg whites into the sweet potato–buttermilk mixture until thoroughly combined. Pour the mixture into the prepared pie crust and bake on the middle rack until the center is firm and set, 35 to 40 minutes.

5. Remove the pie from the oven and cool completely on a rack. Serve at room temperature (or cover with plastic wrap, chill in the refrigerator, and serve cold), with a dollop of whipped cream and a mint leaf on top.

Sweet Pie Crust

This pie crust works well for all kinds of dessert pies. The trick to getting it to bake up nice and flaky is to chill all your ingredients ahead of time in the bowl you're going to be working in. If it's really warm out, we even put our rolling pin in the freezer while the ingredients are chilling. Although some people like to use cake flour in their pie crusts, we like the flavor of all-purpose better.

MAKES 1 PIE SHELL OR 1 TOP (FOR A DOUBLE-CRUST PIE)

TIME: 1 HOUR TO CHILL, 5-8 MINUTES TO PREPARE, 25 MINUTES TO BAKE

1½ cups sifted bleached all-purpose flour, plus more for dusting

1 tablespoon sugar

1 teaspoon salt

4 tablespoons cold lard, cut into small pieces

4 tablespoons cold butter, cut into small pieces

¼ cup ice water

1. Sift the dry ingredients together in a medium bowl. Sprinkle the pieces of lard and butter over them and place the bowl in the refrigerator for 30 minutes. Dust your work surface with flour. If prebaking, preheat the oven to 325 degrees.

2. Using a pastry blender or your fingertips, cut the lard and butter into the dry ingredients until the mixture resembles coarse crumbs, with a scattering of pea-sized pieces throughout. Add ice water a tablespoon at a time, and toss with a fork to combine after each addition, until the pastry holds together when pinched (you may not use all the ice water).

3. Gather the pastry together into a round disk, wrap tightly in plastic wrap, and refrigerate for 15 minutes or until ready to use.

4. With a floured pin, roll out the dough on the floured surface to a 12-inch round. To make a pie shell, transfer to a 9-inch pie pan. Fold any excess dough that hangs below the rim of the pan on top of the rim so you have enough material to crimp. Cut off any egregious excess and use it to patch any holes or tears. Refrigerate for 15 minutes before filling or prebaking.

5. To prebake the crust, lay a sheet of aluminum foil over the dough and carefully scatter pie weights, dried beans, or pennies in the pan. Bake on the middle rack for 12 to 15 minutes. Remove the pie weights and the foil, prick the bottom of the crust with a fork, and bake for 10 minutes more, or until the bottom of the crust appears dry.

The Lees on Lard

Lard just tastes so great in pie crust, and a local butcher can usually get you good lard. But if it's not available, by all means use all butter. We avoid the grocery store lard whipped with BHT (a preservative) at all costs because it does not taste good. We want to get people excited about lard, so we only use the good stuff!

Clover Peach Fried Pies

The Lees on Frying
You can usually reuse your frying oil twice before it starts to break down, turning darker and taking on off odors. After frying, let the oil cool, then pour it through a funnel lined with a coffee filter to strain out any crumbs. Store the oil in the bottle it came in.

Georgia is known as "The Peach State," but even some Georgians we know will admit that the sweetest peaches come from York County, South Carolina, and in particular from the town of Clover, about 4 hours' drive north of Charleston.

The peach—summer's essence, blushing red and orange—is so sublime that being choosy about the type seems absurd. And yet to us, July's Sunhighs, Red Havens, and Georgia Belles are the most flavorful, with a flowery, rosy peachiness that we prefer to June's understated cling varieties (better for canning and cobblers) and August's treacly Blakes, Monroes, and Elbertas.

The Sanders Peach Stand, in tiny Filbert, between Clover and York, is a spartan shed just south of the North Carolina border; it sells all those varieties plus ten others. Dori Sanders, who works the farm's fifty acres with her sister, Virginia, and their brothers, Orestus and Jarvis, may be the only peach farmer in America who has written a novel—*Clover*, set on a peach farm, of course— that has been translated into eight languages and appeared on bestseller lists in Japan. While there are always a starstruck few making the pilgrimage to buy signed copies of her books, locals visit the open-air woodshed for the quality of her ripe peaches.

Though the Sanderses keep trying out new varieties and rotating tree crops every ten to twelve years, they maintain an old orchard, too, for longtime customers who prefer classics like Elbertas and Starlights. And since the stand has no refrigeration (it's the only one in York County without electricity), the peaches are picked twice a day. If you arrive in the late afternoon and they've sold out of your beloved Sunhighs, Dori might ask you to sit a spell beneath a shade tree while she fires up the Massey-Ferguson tractor, drives out to the orchard, and picks you some to order.

These pies are scrumptious little pastry envelopes of velvety filling, cooked down from rehydrated dried peaches with just a hint of spice and a splash of bourbon, but not enough to obscure the ripe flavor of summer peaches. We dehydrate Sanders's July peaches ourselves, and they are wonderful, but any high-quality dried peaches from a reputable market will suffice.

MAKES 12 PIES; ENOUGH FOR 6 PEOPLE

TIME: 1½ HOURS

2¾ cups plus one tablespoon sifted cake flour or 2½ cups sifted
　　bleached all-purpose flour, plus more for dusting surfaces and hands

　1　teaspoon kosher salt

　½　teaspoon baking powder

　4　tablespoons cold butter, cut into ¼-inch dice

　4　tablespoons cold lard, cut into ¼-inch dice
　　　(see The Lees on Lard, page 151)

　¾　cup cold whole milk

　2　cups dried peaches (about 4½ ounces)

　¼　cup packed light brown sugar

　¼　cup Tennessee whiskey or Kentucky bourbon

　½　teaspoon cinnamon

　2　whole cloves

2½ cups peanut oil

　1　tablespoon confectioners' sugar, for garnish

1. Sift the flour, salt, and baking powder together twice. Add the butter and lard and work the mixture with a pastry blender or your fingertips until it resembles coarse crumbs with pea-sized pieces scattered throughout. Add the milk and toss with a fork until the dough comes together when you pinch a small amount between your thumb and forefinger. With floured hands, knead the dough a couple of times. Roll it into 12 equal balls and refrigerate for 30 minutes.

2. In a medium saucepan, bring the peaches and 4 cups water to a boil over high heat. Turn the heat down to low, cover, and simmer vigorously until the peaches are very soft, about 30 minutes. Strain, discard the cooking water, and return the peaches to the pan. Mash with a fork or potato masher. Add the brown sugar, bourbon, cinnamon, and cloves, stir, and simmer over very low heat for 15 minutes more, stirring every 3 minutes, until the peaches are as thick as jam. Remove the cloves and discard.

The Lees on Pie Toppings

We serve these pies with our buttermilk ice cream, but plain vanilla or coconut ice cream would work, too—anything that doesn't pull you away from the flavor of the pies. Or use a spoonful of crème fraîche for a cool, sour contrast.

3. On a floured board, flatten the balls of dough and roll with a floured pin into rounds about 6 inches in diameter and ⅛-inch thick. Place 2 tablespoons peach mixture in the center of each round and brush cold water around the perimeter. Fold the dough over the peach mixture and seal the pie by pressing gently with a fork around the seam. Trim any excess dough.

4. Preheat the oven to 225 degrees. Line a baking sheet or large platter with paper towels.

5. Pour the oil into a 9-inch skillet to a depth of ½ inch. Heat over high heat until the oil reaches 375 degrees on a candy thermometer. Place 4 pies in the skillet and fry, turning them once, for 3 minutes total, until the crusts are golden brown. Transfer the fried pies to the baking sheet lined with paper towels and place in the oven to warm. Repeat with two more batches of pies. When all the pies have been fried, dust them with confectioners' sugar.

6. Serve each guest 2 warm pies, with scoops of ice cream.

best of the best exclusive

Marjoram-Scented Turnip Spoon Bread

6 TO 8 SERVINGS

1½ pounds white turnips, peeled and cut into ½-inch dice

4 tablespoons unsalted butter, melted, plus more for brushing

1½ tablespoons marjoram

Kosher salt and freshly ground pepper

4 large eggs, separated

2 cups whole milk

½ cup water

1 cup cornmeal

1. Butter a 9-inch-square baking dish. In a medium saucepan, steam the turnips over 1 inch of boiling water until very tender, about 20 minutes.

2. Transfer the turnips to a food processor. Add the butter and marjoram and puree until smooth, about 1 minute. Transfer the puree to a large bowl and season generously with salt and pepper. Whisk in the egg yolks.

3. Preheat the oven to 375°. In a large saucepan, bring the milk and the water to a simmer over moderate heat. Slowly pour in the cornmeal, whisking constantly, until smooth. Cook over moderately low heat until thick, about 2 minutes. Remove from the heat and let stand for 5 minutes. Whisk the cornmeal into the turnip mixture until blended.

4. In a medium bowl, using an electric mixer, beat the egg whites at medium speed until soft peaks form. Using a rubber spatula, fold the egg whites into the turnip mixture until no streaks remain. Scrape the spoon bread batter into the prepared baking dish and bake for about 45 minutes, until puffed and lightly browned. Serve warm.

Editor's Note

The Lee brothers explain that spoon bread is like a cornmeal soufflé. Feel free to substitute parsnips and chives, or sweet potatoes and leeks, for the turnips and marjoram.

The Pizza Maker's Wife's
Pan-Fried Steaks, p. 158

Lobel's Meat and Wine

By Stanley, Leon, Evan, Mark & David Lobel

"We're butchers, so maybe we understand more about cuts of meat than a chef does," says Mark Lobel, a member of the fifth generation at his family's eponymous Manhattan shop. Putting both their cleavers and corkscrews to good use, the Lobel men created recipes for every type of meat imaginable, even game birds and offal, along with smart advice on the best wines for pairing. What to have with their intensely flavorful Marinated Rib Steaks with Garlic-Parsley Butter? A Pinot Noir from Burgundy's Côte Chalonnais.

With Mary Goodbody and David Whiteman; published by Chronicle Books, $35. Find more recipes by the Lobels at foodandwine.com/lobel

The Pizza Maker's Wife's Pan-Fried Steaks

Bistecca alla Pizzaiola

The Lobels on Tomatoes

Use the best-quality canned tomatoes you can find, because they make a difference in this dish. If they're available, we recommend San Marzano. Muir Glen organic whole tomatoes are also excellent.

Bathing a tender, well-browned steak in tomato sauce may strike some as odd, but with this classic dish from Campania, Italy, the results are delicious. The oregano-scented tomato sauce can be prepared up to two days earlier and refrigerated. Besides using good-quality steaks and canned tomatoes, the trick to getting this simple dish just right is to brown the steaks deeply in a very hot skillet while leaving them slightly undone in the center so they finish cooking in the tomato sauce. Try this steak with sautéed zucchini or eggplant—alone or in combination—served on the side. Together, these flavors evoke the direct and exceptional cooking of Naples.

WINE NOTE The most sympathetic wines for tomato sauce are found by following the principle "like goes with like." That is, since tomato sauce is acidic and fruity, your wine choice should be either nicely acidic, somewhat fruity, or both. For us, that means you can match the acidity of the sauce by serving a simple, tangy (acidic) Chianti, or match its fruitiness by serving warm, darkly fruity Montepulciano d'Abruzzo. Two favorites: Fattoria di Lucignano Chianti Colli Fiorentini and Barone Cornacchia Montepulciano d'Abruzzo.

SERVES 2

Two 10- to 11-ounce strip steaks (on or off the bone), each about 1 inch thick, trimmed of excess fat

5 tablespoons extra-virgin olive oil

4 large cloves garlic, finely chopped

One 28-ounce can peeled whole tomatoes, drained with ¾ cup juice reserved, and finely chopped

Kosher salt

Generous pinch of crushed red pepper flakes

1½ teaspoons finely chopped fresh oregano or ½ teaspoon dried

Freshly ground black pepper

½ cup dry white wine

1 tablespoon finely chopped fresh flat-leaf parsley

1. Let the steaks come to room temperature while you make the tomato sauce.

2. In a saucepan, heat 3 tablespoons of the olive oil and cook the garlic over medium-low heat until pale golden at the edges, 3 to 4 minutes.

3. Add the tomatoes and reserved juice, raise the heat, and bring to a simmer. Stir in ½ teaspoon salt and the crushed red pepper flakes and simmer gently for 20 minutes.

4. Stir in the oregano and a few generous grindings of black pepper and simmer until the sauce has thickened but is still somewhat fluid, about 5 to 10 minutes longer. Remove from the heat and set aside.

5. Salt the steaks well on both sides. Turn on the stove vent if you have one.

6. In a large, heavy skillet, heat the remaining 2 tablespoons olive oil over medium-high heat. When it just begins to smoke, swirl the oil to coat the bottom of the skillet and cook the steaks until nicely browned on both sides but still a good deal rarer in the middle than you prefer to eat them (that is, slightly raw), 2½ to 3½ minutes per side. Transfer to a plate and set aside.

7. Let the skillet cool slightly and then place over medium heat. Add the wine and simmer until reduced by half, scraping the bottom of the skillet to loosen any browned bits, 2 to 3 minutes.

8. Gently reheat the tomato sauce and add it to the skillet with the reduced wine, along with any accumulated juices from the steaks. Stir to incorporate.

9. Return the steaks to the skillet and spoon enough sauce over them to cover. Simmer gently until the steaks are cooked to your liking, 3 to 4 minutes for medium-rare.

10. Transfer the steaks to warmed serving plates. The sauce should be thickened but still a little fluid. If necessary, simmer the sauce for a few moments more to thicken, or thin it with 1 or 2 tablespoons water. Top the steaks with tomato sauce, garnish with the parsley, and serve.

Marinated Rib Steaks with Garlic-Parsley Butter
Steak Chalonnais

Editor's Note

Rib steaks are a buttery cut, so marinating isn't necessary to tenderize them. The brief time that these steaks spend in a mix of wine, shallot and oil simply infuses them with extra flavor.

Rich, full-flavored garlic-parsley butter is a favorite in Burgundy and for very good reason: How else could the French have convinced so many people from all corners of the globe to devour snails? It's equally lovely spooned over rib steaks, which, cut from the rib section, are a little fattier and have bolder beef flavor than steaks cut from the loin.

WINE NOTE We found that any medium-bodied Pinot Noir from the Côte Chalonnais that isn't too marked by the flavors of new oak barrels is spot-on with this dish, and all of them tasted particularly good when served cool or at cool room temperature. Paul Jacqueson's Rully 1er Cru "Les Clous" was a standout in our tasting, but there's an abundance of food-friendly wine produced in the Côte Chalonnais, wines usually a little lighter on their feet than the region's more famous cousin, the Côte d'Or, to the north. Also look for wines from Mercurey, Givry, and Montagny or serve a good-quality Bourgogne rouge. From the New World wine regions, look for producers of lighter-weight and more delicate Pinot Noir, whether from Oregon, California, New Zealand, or elsewhere. One regionally chauvinistic favorite: Millbrook Pinot Noir from New York's Hudson Valley.

SERVES 2

- 1 cup medium-bodied Pinot Noir
- 1 large shallot, thinly sliced

Freshly ground black pepper

- 6 tablespoons vegetable oil

Two 10- or 11-ounce rib or strip steaks (on or off the bone), each about ¾ inch thick, trimmed of excess fat

- ¼ cup unsalted butter, at room temperature
- ½ teaspoon minced garlic
- 2 tablespoons finely chopped fresh flat-leaf parsley
- 1 teaspoon all-purpose flour

Kosher salt

1. In a small saucepan, bring the wine to a boil over medium-high heat. Reduce the heat to medium and simmer until reduced by one-fourth (to ¾ cup), about 4 minutes. Let cool slightly.

2. In a glass, ceramic, or other nonreactive dish just large enough to hold the steaks, whisk together the reduced wine, the shallot, and a few generous grindings of pepper. Whisk in 3 tablespoons of the oil. Add the steaks and turn a few times to coat. Marinate at room temperature for 1 to 2 hours, turning and basting every so often. Refrigerate if marinating any longer than this.

3. Meanwhile, in a small bowl, mash together the butter, garlic, parsley, flour, a pinch of salt, and a few grindings of pepper until well combined. Shape into 4 tablespoon-sized rounds, put on a small plate, cover, and refrigerate.

4. Remove the steaks from the marinade, reserving the marinade. Blot the steaks lightly with a paper towel to remove excess moisture and sprinkle generously with salt.

5. Preheat a heavy skillet over medium-high heat until almost smoking. Carefully add the remaining 3 tablespoons oil and swirl the oil to coat the bottom of the skillet. Add the steaks and cook for about 3 minutes per side for medium-rare.

6. Transfer the steaks to serving plates and pour off any fat in the skillet. Keep the steaks warm in a very low (200°F) oven.

7. Let the skillet cool for about 30 seconds and then place over medium heat. Add the reserved marinade and cook until reduced by half, scraping the bottom of the skillet to loosen any browned bits. Remove from the heat and whisk in the garlic-parsley butter, 1 piece at a time, until smooth. Spoon the sauce over the steaks and serve immediately.

Pork Cutlets with Apples, Onions, and Marjoram
Scweinsmedallions mit Marjoran

The Lobels on Thinking Ahead

The key to success in this dish is to have all the ingredients and equipment at hand before you start to fry. Because the cutlets cook quickly, this allows you to focus on getting them in and out of the pan before they're overcooked.

This dish displays the excellent cooking traits of good-quality German Riesling wine, which is not surprising considering the preparation originated in Germany's Rhineland. While it's relatively simple and quick to put together, it nevertheless boasts vibrant and complex flavor, due in part to the gentle sweetness, balance, and perfume of these wines. To double the recipe, use two skillets.

WINE NOTE German Riesling! For those who aren't familiar with it, here's a chance to learn about the most refined and nimble food wine there is. From the Rheingau, the Joseph Leitz Rüdesheimer Klosterlay Kabinett is a sweet-tart style of Riesling that sumptuously complements the pork in a creamy and expressive style. But it's the slightly dryer *halbtrocken* style of Riesling that really makes the match take off. From the Rheinpfalz: Lingenfelder's Freisenheimer Musikantenbuckel Kabinett Halbtrocken.

SERVES 2

¾ cup off-dry Riesling wine

¼ cup golden raisins

About 1¼ cups vegetable oil

1 large yellow onion, thinly sliced

2 sweet apples such as Gala or Fuji, peeled, cored, halved and cut into thin, half-moon slices

¾ cup pork stock, Chicken Stock (recipe follows), or canned low-sodium chicken broth

3 teaspoons finely chopped fresh marjoram

Kosher salt

1 pound boneless pork loin, cut into 6 slices (cutlets), each about ⅜ inch thick, at room temperature

Freshly ground black pepper

All-purpose flour for dredging

2 tablespoons whole-grain or smooth German-style mustard such as Inglehoffer's

The Lobels on Pork

We highly recommend Kurobuta pork, which comes from purebred Berkshire pigs. It's juicy, with more marbling than most breeds, and it has a lush, distinctive, abundant flavor—more like pork used to be.

1. In a small saucepan, bring the wine and raisins to a simmer over medium-high heat. Reduce the heat so that the wine simmers gently and cook until reduced by half, about 4 minutes. Set aside.

2. In a large skillet, heat ¼ cup of the oil over medium heat and cook the onion slices, stirring occasionally, until softened and pale gold at the edges, 8 to 10 minutes. Stir in the apples and cook for 5 minutes more. Add the wine-raisin mixture, the stock, 2 teaspoons of the marjoram, and ¾ teaspoon salt and bring to a simmer.

3. Reduce the heat to medium low and simmer gently until the liquid has reduced by two-thirds but the mixture is still slightly liquid, 5 to 7 minutes. Set aside.

4. Preheat the oven to 200°F. Sprinkle the pork slices on both sides generously with salt and lightly with pepper. Put about 1 cup of flour on a large plate.

5. In a large skillet, pour enough oil to reach a depth of about ¼ inch and heat over medium heat. While the oil heats, spread both sides of each pork slice with mustard and then dredge with the flour. Shake off the excess flour and when the oil begins to smoke carefully slide 2 to 3 pork slices into the skillet. Reduce the heat slightly and fry for 1½ to 2 minutes per side. The pork slices will be barely pink in the center. Transfer to a paper towel–lined plate and keep warm in the oven. Repeat to fry the remaining pork slices, letting the oil get hot again between batches.

6. Gently rewarm the reserved onion-apple mixture over low heat. Divide the mixture between 2 serving plates and top each with 3 pork cutlets. Garnish with the remaining 1 teaspoon marjoram and serve immediately.

Lobel's Meat
and Wine
*By Stanley, Leon, Evan,
Mark & David Lobel*

Chicken Stock

MAKES ABOUT 6 CUPS

- 3 pounds chicken wings, cut into 3 or 4 pieces each
- 8 cups cold water
- ½ large onion, halved
- ½ carrot, peeled and halved
- ½ stalk celery, halved
- 2 large cloves garlic, crushed
- 2 sprigs fresh thyme
- ½ bay leaf
- ¼ teaspoon salt

1. In a stock pot, combine the chicken wings with the water and bring to a simmer over medium high heat. As it comes to a simmer, skim off any foam that rises to the surface with a ladle or large spoon.

2. Add the onion, carrot, celery, garlic, thyme, bay leaf, and salt. Cook, uncovered, at a gentle simmer, stirring occasionally, for 1 hour.

3. Remove from the heat and let the stock rest for 15 minutes. Strain through a large fine-mesh strainer or a colander lined with a double layer of damp cheesecloth into a large bowl.

4. Fill a larger bowl or the sink with ice and water and nest the bowl of broth in it. Stir regularly until the broth has cooled.

5. Transfer to airtight containers and refrigerate for up to 3 days, or freeze for up to 3 months.

Editor's Note

Using chicken wings results in a stock full of gelatin, which gives the broth body and rich flavor. Because the wings also release a lot of fat, it's best to make this stock in advance so you can refrigerate it overnight. Once chilled, the liquid will gel and the fat will lift off easily.

Chicken Gratin with Onion Sauce and Gruyère

Le Poulet Gaston Gérard

The Lobels on Chicken

Whenever possible, choose fresh chicken over frozen—it's moister and more flavorful. If you buy it vacuum-packed, check for water in the package, which indicates that the bird may have been frozen.

WINE NOTE Cheese and cream can be tough on wines, especially reds, and so it surprised us to find that the level of a red wine was dropping quickly in our glasses alongside the chicken gratin (more proof, if any were needed, that even the few wine "rules" you think are worth abiding by can crumble right before you). Our favorite among a range of wines was a ready-to-drink medium-weight red Burgundy with a gentle core of earthy, red fruit flavors: the Bouchard Père et Fils Santenay. A Pinot Noir from Oregon like the Adelsheim Pinot Noir from the Willamette Valley would be a kindred choice from the United States.

SERVES 4

Kosher salt

One 3½- to 4-pound chicken, cut into 8 serving pieces
    (see Butcher's Note, page 168)

2 tablespoons vegetable oil

2 tablespoons unsalted butter

2 yellow onions, finely chopped

¾ cup finely chopped shallots

1¼ cups dry white wine such as Bourgogne blanc

½ cup crème fraîche

4 tablespoons Dijon mustard

5 ounces Gruyère cheese, coarsely grated

1. Generously salt the chicken on all sides. In a large sauté pan, heat the oil and butter over medium-high heat until the butter melts. Working in two batches if necessary, cook the chicken until rich golden brown all over, 10 to 12 minutes per batch, reducing the heat if it threatens to burn. (To avoid overcooking them, remove any thinner breast pieces just before they're cooked through.) Transfer to a plate, tent loosely with aluminum foil, and place in a very low (200°F) oven.

2. Pour off all but about 4 tablespoons of the fat and place the pan over medium heat. Add the onions and shallots and cook, stirring occasionally,

until pale gold at the edges, 8 to 10 minutes. Raise the heat to medium-high and add the wine. Simmer for 2 minutes, scraping the bottom of the pan to loosen any browned bits.

3. Return the legs and thighs to the skillet along with any accumulated juices. Cook at a bare simmer for 10 minutes, turning the pieces after about 5 minutes. Add the breast pieces and cook for 5 minutes longer. Check to make sure all the chicken is just cooked through. Transfer the chicken to a plate.

4. Whisk the crème fraîche, mustard, and 1 teaspoon of salt into the pan juices until well mixed.

5. Preheat the broiler.

6. Evenly distribute half the cheese over the bottom of an earthenware or glass baking dish just large enough to hold the chicken in a single layer. Arrange the chicken on top of the cheese. Pour all the onion sauce evenly over the chicken and top with the rest of the cheese.

7. Broil until bubbly and just a little golden in spots. Serve immediately from the baking dish, spooning additional onion sauce over each portion.

BUTCHER'S NOTE We recommend you cut up a whole chicken to get the 8 pieces called for here—2 semi-boneless breast halves, each cut in half to make 4 pieces; 2 thighs; and 2 drumsticks. With the bird breast-side up, slit the skin between the thighs and breast, pull the thighs away, and cut through the exposed ball-and-socket joint. Then, cut each leg in half through the joint between the thigh and drumstick. Next, remove the first two wing joints attached to the breast (reserve these and the carcass for stock). To remove the breast halves, cut straight down along one side of the breastbone— its entire length—until the knife meets the rib cage. Then, begin drawing the knife toward you in long strokes where the breast meat meets the ribs, gradually separating the breast meat from the curve of the ribs and "peeling" the breast away from the ribs with your free hand as you cut. Spin the bird around 180 degrees and repeat with the second breast half. Cut each half again crosswise to make 4 pieces of breast meat.

Lobel's Meat
and Wine
*By Stanley, Leon, Evan,
Mark & David Lobel*

best of the best exclusive
Puerto Rican Soupy Rice

6 SERVINGS

Editor's Note

Known as *asopao,* one of Puerto Rico's national dishes, this hearty, soupy stew is sometimes likened to gumbo. This savory recipe will appear in the Lobel's next cookbook, tentatively titled *Lobel's Meat Bible* (Chronicle Books, 2008).

- 15 green olives, pitted and coarsely chopped
- 2 teaspoons chopped fresh oregano
- 2 teaspoons finely grated lime zest, plus lime wedges for serving
- ¼ cup chopped cilantro
- 1 tablespoon minced garlic

Kosher salt and freshly ground pepper

- 6 tablespoons extra-virgin olive oil

1¼ pounds skinless, boneless chicken thighs, cut into 1-inch pieces

- 1 onion, cut into ¼-inch dice
- 2 jalapeños, seeded and minced
- 2 ounces smoked ham, cut into ½-inch dice

One 15-ounce can whole tomatoes, drained and coarsely chopped

- 6 cups chicken stock or low-sodium broth
- ⅔ cup long-grain white rice, rinsed
- ½ butternut squash (14 ounces)—peeled, seeded and cut into ½-inch dice
- ¼ pound green beans, cut into ½-inch lengths
- 1 roasted red bell pepper from a jar, cut into 1-by-½-inch strips

1. In a bowl, mix the olives, oregano, lime zest, 3 tablespoons of the cilantro, 1 teaspoon of garlic, 2 teaspoons of kosher salt and ¼ teaspoon of pepper. Stir in 3 tablespoons of olive oil. Add the chicken and toss. Let stand for 30 minutes.

2. In a large soup pot, heat the remaining 3 tablespoons of oil. Add the onion, jalapeños and the remaining 2 teaspoons of garlic and cook over moderate heat until the onion is softened, 5 minutes. Add the ham and tomatoes and cook for 3 minutes. Add the stock and bring to a boil. Stir in the rice and cook over moderately high heat for 2 minutes. Add the squash and green beans and simmer for 10 minutes, or until the rice is almost tender. Add the chicken and marinade and simmer until the chicken is cooked through, about 5 minutes. Stir in the roasted pepper; season with salt and pepper. Ladle into bowls, sprinkle with the remaining cilantro and serve with lime wedges.

Spaghetti Fritters, p. 172

Jamie's Italy

By Jamie Oliver

Television personality Jamie Oliver has loved Italy since his days as a sous-chef at London's iconic Italian restaurant, The River Café. This stunning book, which doubles as a travelogue, is an intense and page-turning look at Italian food (and the cooks, artisans and farmers who produce it). Accompanying the more than 120 delicious and accessible recipes are playful snapshots of Oliver crisscrossing the country—playing soccer with village boys or sharing risotto with a wizened shepherd.

Published by Hyperion, $34.95.
Find more recipes by Jamie Oliver at foodandwine.com/oliver

Spaghetti Fritters
Frittelle di Spaghetti

Editor's Note

Oliver likes to dress up these fritters by adding 2 roughly chopped anchovies and 1 to 2 crumbled dried chiles to the egg mixture.

I've seen fried pasta dishes before, but never thought all that much about them until I saw Giovanni, who runs a restaurant on the island of Marettimo, just off the coast of Sicily, fry me a spaghetti fritter and serve it in a very unusual way. He put it in a bowl with some broth and boiled pork from a bollito misto. Absolutely amazing. The broth made it go soggy but it was still beautiful to eat. But the great thing about fried pasta is its portability. Once you've got the base recipe you can vary the flavor in different ways. For instance, I'm totally obsessed by chile, so I always add that to mine. Basically you bind the pasta with a little egg and season it with key Italian ingredients like parsley and Parmesan (but don't be tempted to use pre-grated Parmesan— it will taste horrible). From there you can add little flakes of fish, a sprinkling of chile, or little chopped-up tomatoes or olives. When it's cooked, the fritter should be soft in the middle and crunchy on the outside—fandabidozi!

MAKES 4

2 cloves of garlic, peeled and finely chopped

A handful of fresh flat-leaf parsley, finely chopped

2 eggs plus 1 yolk, preferably organic

2 handfuls of freshly grated Parmesan cheese

Sea salt and freshly ground black pepper

7 ounces dried spaghetti

Olive oil

Put all your ingredients, apart from the spaghetti and olive oil, into a bowl and mix together. Add your spaghetti to a pan of salted, boiling water and cook according to the package instructions. Drain the pasta in a colander and rinse under cold water to cool it down. Once the pasta is cool, snip it with scissors into pieces roughly 3 inches long and add them to the bowl. Mix well.

Pour a little oil into a pan and place on the heat. Then, using a fork, add piles (as big or as small as you like) of the spaghetti mixture to the pan and fry until golden and crisp on both sides. Sometimes it's delicious to fry the fritters in a slightly hotter pan so they are really golden outside but soft and warm inside.

Chicken and Mushroom Pasta Bake

Spaghetti Tetrazzini

I remember meeting a lovely old couple outside my parents' pub and when they heard I was going to Italy they told me to make sure I cooked turkey tetrazzini—I hadn't a clue what they were talking about and then, by chance, I saw a recipe for chicken tetrazzini in an old Italian cookbook and it's great—really tacky but gorgeous! Here's my version...

SERVES 4

1 ounce/a small handful of dried porcini mushrooms

Olive oil

4 chicken thighs, boned, skinned, and cut into bite-sized pieces

Sea salt and freshly ground black pepper

2 cloves of garlic, peeled and finely sliced

2 handfuls of mixed fresh mushrooms, cleaned and torn

1 cup white wine

1 pound dried spaghetti

2¼ cups heavy cream

7 ounces Parmesan cheese, grated

A sprig of fresh basil, leaves picked

Extra virgin olive oil

Preheat the oven to 400°F. Put your porcini mushrooms in a bowl and pour just enough boiling water over to cover them (approx. ⅔ cup). Put to one side to soak for a few minutes. Heat a saucepan big enough to hold all the ingredients, and pour in a splash of olive oil. Season the chicken pieces with salt and pepper and brown them gently in the oil. Strain the porcini, reserving the soaking water, and add them to the pan with the garlic and fresh mushrooms. Add the wine, with the strained porcini soaking water, and turn the heat down. Simmer gently until the chicken pieces are cooked through and the wine has reduced a little.

Oliver on Mushrooms

Dried mushrooms add a deep, meaty flavor to a dish. In place of the porcini in this recipe, you can try other types like chanterelles or morels.

Meanwhile, cook the spaghetti in plenty of boiling salted water according to the package instructions and drain well. Add the cream to the pan of chicken, then bring to a boil and turn the heat off. Season well with salt and freshly ground black pepper. Add the drained spaghetti to the creamy chicken sauce and toss well. Add three-quarters of the Parmesan and all of the basil and stir well. Transfer to an ovenproof baking dish or nonstick pan, sprinkle with half the remaining cheese, and bake in the oven until golden brown, bubbling, and crisp. Divide between your plates, drizzle with extra virgin olive oil, and sprinkle with the rest of the cheese before serving.

Cauliflower Risotto
Risotto ai Cavolfiori

This is an absolutely delicious recipe. It's quite unusual, and the best thing about it is that it makes a hero of the much-underloved everyday cauliflower. If you're down at the farmers' market, or at the supermarket, have a look around for a Romanesco cauliflower—it's a similar size to a normal cauliflower but spiky and green. It also has a delicious flavor. The reason I love this dish is because it takes some all-time classic ingredients and puts them together in a great way. In Britain we normally eat cauliflower baked with cheese, and in Italy it is baked as a parmigiana with cream, cheese, and anchovies. All these flavors are in this risotto, with the added bonus of really crunchy chile *pangrattato* sprinkled on top—it gives an amazing kick.

SERVES 6

- 2 handfuls of stale bread, torn into pieces
- 1 small can of anchovies, oil from can reserved
- 3 small dried red chiles

Extra virgin olive oil

- 1 cauliflower
- 1 risotto bianco (recipe follows)

A handful of chopped fresh parsley

Sea salt and freshly ground black pepper

Parmesan cheese, for grating

Whiz the bread in a food processor with the anchovies, the oil from the can, and the chiles. Heat a frying pan with a splash of oil and fry the flavored breadcrumbs, stirring and tossing constantly until golden brown.

Trim the coarse leaves off the cauliflower and cut out the stalk. Chop the nice inner part of the stalk finely. Start making your risotto bianco, adding the chopped cauliflower stalk to the pan with the onion and celery at Stage 1. Add the cauliflower florets to your pan of hot stock.

Continue to follow the basic risotto recipe, adding the stock bit by bit until the rice is half-cooked. By now the cauliflower florets should be quite soft, so you can start to add them to the risotto with the stock, crushing them into

Oliver on Anchovies

Don't think of anchovies as a star ingredient, but as a natural, salty seasoning that adds to the flavor of a dish. If you can taste them strongly, you've added too many.

the rice as you go. Continue until the rice is cooked and all the cauliflower has been added.

At Stage 4, when you add the butter and Parmesan, stir in the parsley, taste, and season. Sprinkle with the anchovy *pangrattato*, grate some more Parmesan over the top, and serve. So, so good!

White Risotto
Risotto Bianco

This is a great basic recipe—it can be stretched in so many different ways to turn it into fantastically flavored risottos.

SERVES 6

- 2 pints stock (chicken, fish, or vegetable, as appropriate)
- 2 tablespoons olive oil

A dollop of butter

- 1 large onion, peeled and finely chopped
- 2 cloves of garlic, peeled and finely chopped
- ½ a head of celery, trimmed and finely chopped
- 2 cups risotto (Arborio) rice
- 2 wineglasses of dry white vermouth (dry Martini or Noilly Prat) or dry white wine

Sea salt and freshly ground black pepper

- 5 tablespoons butter
- 4 ounces freshly grated Parmesan cheese

STAGE 1: Heat the stock. Put the olive oil and butter into a separate pan, add the onion, garlic, and celery, and cook very slowly for about 15 minutes without coloring. This is called a *soffrito*. When the vegetables have softened, add the rice and turn up the heat.

Cauliflower Risotto

STAGE 2: The rice will now begin to lightly fry, so keep stirring it. After a minute it will look slightly translucent. Add the vermouth or wine and keep stirring—it will smell fantastic. Any harsh alcohol flavors will evaporate and leave the rice with a tasty essence.

STAGE 3: Once the vermouth or wine has cooked into the rice, add your first ladle of hot stock and a good pinch of salt. Turn the heat down to a simmer so the rice doesn't cook too quickly on the outside. Keep adding ladlefuls of stock, stirring and massaging the creamy starch out of the rice, allowing each ladleful to be absorbed before adding the next. This will take around 15 minutes. Taste the rice to check if it's cooked. If not, carry on adding stock until the rice is soft but with a slight bite. Don't forget to check the seasoning carefully. If you run out of stock before the rice is cooked, add some boiling water.

STAGE 4: Remove from the heat and add the butter and Parmesan. Stir well. Place a lid on the pan and allow to sit for 2 minutes. This is the most important part of making the perfect risotto, as this is when it becomes amazingly creamy and oozy like it should be. Eat it as soon as possible, while it retains its beautiful texture.

Pork Chops with Sage
Costolette di Maiale con Salvia

Pork chops are a pretty regular occurrence in Italy. They can be cooked in many, many ways, but this recipe is one of my favorites. When I first saw it being made in a trattoria in Florence, on my first-ever trip to Italy, the young lady who was making it inserted a small paring knife into the side of the chops and moved it from side to side to create a little pocket inside the meat. It was clever, as you couldn't tell from the outside that this "flavor pocket" was there. A little pork fat or butter can be rubbed inside the pocket and then you can add some prosciutto fat, or smashed-up chestnuts or walnuts (depending on what's in season). A little fresh sage should always be added, and maybe a little garlic. I like to add a tiny amount of lemon zest as well, as it's best friends with pork. Have a go at trying this pocket trick.

Oliver on Pancetta
I prefer pancetta to bacon because it has more flavor and contains less water, so I find I can use less of it.

SERVES 4

2½ pounds all-purpose potatoes, peeled and diced

Sea salt and freshly ground black pepper

 4 thick pork chops, on the bone

24 fresh sage leaves

 1 bulb of garlic

 4 slices of prosciutto

 4 tablespoons butter, finely diced

 4 dried apricots

Extra virgin olive oil

Flour

 6 thick strips of pancetta or bacon (½ inch thick, if possible),
    or an 8-ounce package of pancetta lardons

Preheat the oven to 425°F. Put your potatoes into a pot of salted water and bring to a boil. Boil 3 or 4 minutes—you only want to parboil them—then drain and allow to steam dry. Lay your pork chops on a board and insert a small paring knife horizontally into the side of each chop to make a hidden pocket. Make sure the tip of your knife stays in the middle of the chop, as you don't want to cut through the meat to either side. Be careful—watch your fingers!

Pork Chops with Sage

Set aside 8 of the largest sage leaves. Add 8 more leaves to your food processor with a peeled clove of garlic, the prosciutto, butter, apricots, and a pinch of salt and pepper and give it a whiz. This is now a beautifully flavored butter that can be divided between the pork chops and pushed into the pockets.

Dress the 8 large sage leaves that you set aside with a little oil and press one side of them into some flour. Press a leaf, flour side down, onto each side of the chops (so you have 2 leaves on each chop). Leave the chops on a plate, covered with plastic wrap, to come to room temperature while you get your potatoes ready.

If you're using thick strips of pancetta, slice them into matchsticks, as thick as a pencil. Put them into a large roasting pan, with your potatoes, the remaining sage leaves, and the rest of your whole unpeeled garlic cloves. Drizzle with a little extra virgin olive oil and put the pan into the preheated oven. After 10 minutes, put a frying pan on the burner and get it very hot. Add a touch of olive oil and put in your seasoned pork chops. Fry for 10 minutes, until golden and crisp on both sides, then remove the pan of potatoes from the oven—they should be nice and light golden by now—and place the chops on top. Put the pan back into the oven for 10–15 minutes, depending on how thick the chops are, then remove the pan from the oven and serve.

Chile-Garlic Peanuts, p. 184

Big Small Plates

By Cindy Pawlcyn with Pablo Jacinto & Erasto Jacinto

Napa Valley chef Cindy Pawlcyn (of Mustard's Grill in Yountville and Cindy's Backstreet Kitchen and Go Fish, both in St. Helena) says starters are some of the most popular items on her menus. That helps explain why Pawlcyn, along with co-chefs and partners Pablo Jacinto and Erasto Jacinto, wrote *Big Small Plates*, with recipes that she says are "big in taste and small in size." And, of course, powerfully flavored dishes like crispy Black Pepper and Garlic Chicken Wings make fabulous main courses if you double the recipe.

Published by Ten Speed Press, $35.
Find more recipes by Cindy Pawlcyn at foodandwine.com/pawlcyn

Chile-Garlic Peanuts

Pawlcyn on Unpeeled Garlic

Frying unpeeled garlic cloves keeps them from burning. The papery skins protect them but allow their garlicky flavor to come through.

The peanuts you want for this traditional Oaxacan bar snack are the short round guys with red skin that are known as Spanish peanuts. The American peanut is a bit longer than the Spanish peanut and has a brownish skin. It will work, too; it just doesn't quite have the look. For the chiles, any small hot dried chile will do, but I especially like *chiles de árbol* or *chiles pequín* for this.

Traditionally these are cooked in pork lard. Although we *norteños* eat them like crazy when we go south of the border, few of us cook with lard at home anymore. A peanut or vegetable oil would work well also. You just need something with a high smoke point, because you want the oil really hot when the peanuts, chiles, and garlic hit it. I often use a double-handled pan to make shaking the nuts easier as they're cooking. A wok would also work.

Two pounds of peanuts may sound like a lot, but I guarantee the whole batch will disappear quickly, especially if you serve them warm. You can make them in two batches if it is easier for you.

MAKES A BIG BOWLFUL

- 2 whole heads garlic
- ¼ cup peanut or vegetable oil
- 2 pounds shelled raw Spanish peanuts, with skins
- 2 to 4 fiery-hot dried chiles, slightly crushed
- 1 tablespoon kosher salt

Grated zest and juice of 1 lime

Separate the heads of garlic into cloves. Trim off the root ends, but don't peel the cloves. Put the oil in a pan large enough to hold everything, and heat it until it is almost rippling. Add the peanuts, garlic, and chiles; cook, stirring and shaking continuously, for 10 to 12 minutes, until the peanuts have darkened. Add the salt and lime zest and juice to the pan and give it another good stir and shake. Pour out into a serving bowl and watch them go!

Colombian-Style Pork Empanadas

Just about every country in the world has its own kind of baked filled pastry. The Chinese have *bao*, the English have Cornish pasties, Italy has calzones, Russia has pierogis, and the Spanish-influenced countries have empanadas. Most empanadas have savory meat, cheese, or fish fillings, but there are sweet fruit-filled empanadas, too.

The pastry for empanadas can be like a bread dough, or it can resemble a pie crust. The dough in this recipe is very flaky and easy to work with. It can be made ahead and kept refrigerated up to 24 hours, or you can even freeze it and pull it out to use months later (it will keep at least two months). I usually make the dough with butter, because it's handier. When I feel like treating myself I use lard, which is more traditional, makes a flakier pastry, and is extra-delicious. This recipe uses a combination of the two. I really don't feel good about using vegetable shortening, however, because of the current research on how bad trans fats are for us.

Making empanadas takes a bit of work, but the results are well worth the effort. Since the empanadas freeze so well, you could always double the recipe and stash some in the freezer for another day. If you end up with extra filling, it would be great worked into a paella, used as a stuffing for roasted chiles, or in omelettes or enchiladas.

SERVES 6 TO 8 (MAKES 24 TO 32, DEPENDING ON SIZE)

EMPANADA DOUGH

- 2 cups flour
- ½ teaspoon salt
- ½ cup chilled butter, cut into small pieces
- 4 tablespoons lard, frozen and cut into small pieces
- 1 large egg
- 1 large egg yolk
- 4 tablespoons ice water

Pawlcyn on Pork

Boneless shoulder or Boston butt is a tough cut with great flavor. Chopping it into small pieces helps it become tender when cooked. If you'd prefer, you can substitute meat from pork chops or thin-cut pork loin.

FILLING

8 ounces boneless pork shoulder or Boston butt

1 tablespoon olive or vegetable oil

½ onion, minced

½ pasilla chile or green bell pepper, stemmed, seeded, and minced

1½ teaspoons minced garlic

1 tomato, peeled and chopped

1½ teaspoons chopped pimiento-stuffed green olives

1½ teaspoons capers, rinsed and finely chopped

1½ teaspoons raisins, chopped

¼ to ½ teaspoon salt

¼ teaspoon freshly ground black pepper

¼ cup dry sherry

1 small hard-boiled egg, chopped

To make the dough, combine the flour, salt, butter, and lard in a mixer bowl. Using the paddle attachment of an electric mixer or (if by hand) a pastry blender, cut the butter and lard into the dry ingredients until the mixture resembles coarse meal. In a separate bowl, combine the egg, egg yolk, and water; beat lightly. Pour this into the flour mixture and combine quickly, being very careful not to overmix. Stop just before the dough actually comes together completely, and finish it with a few pats by hand. Form the dough into a ball, wrap it in plastic wrap, and flatten it to a 1-inch-thick disk. Chill for at least 1 hour (and up to overnight).

To make the filling, trim the meat of any fat, gristle, or tough sinew. Finely chop it by hand, or you could run it through on the coarse blade of a meat grinder. If you choose to do that, make sure the grinder and the meat are both very cold before you start. Heat the oil in a large skillet over medium-high heat. When hot, add the onion and chile; cook 2 or 3 minutes, until soft. Add the garlic and cook a minute more. Next, stir in the pork and continue cooking till it is no longer pink, 3 to 5 minutes. Add the tomato, olives, capers, raisins, ¼ teaspoon salt, pepper, and sherry. Continue cooking until the liquid has almost completely evaporated. Taste and add more salt, if needed. Allow the mixture to cool completely, then add the egg and mix well. Set the filling aside.

About 10 minutes before you are ready to fill the empanadas, remove the dough from the fridge. Frozen dough should be allowed to defrost overnight in the refrigerator first. In either case, the dough should be cold when you work with it. Roll out the dough on a lightly floured surface to a ¼-inch thickness. Cut out circles using a 4-inch round pastry cutter. You can chill the scraps for 10 minutes, then gently combine them and roll them out again. Don't use the scraps again, though, as the dough will get tough.

To fill the empanadas, place 1½ tablespoons of filling just off center on each dough circle, leaving room around the edges for sealing. Fold into half-moons and crimp the edges with your fingers. The empanadas can be baked right away, or you can freeze them and finish them later. To freeze, place them on a baking sheet and put them in the freezer. When frozen solid, put them in freezer bags and return them to the freezer. Use them up within 4 weeks, if you can.

To bake the empanadas, preheat the oven to 400°F. Bake on an ungreased baking sheet for 25 to 30 minutes, until golden brown. Frozen empanadas will take an extra 10 to 15 minutes; they should go straight from the freezer to the hot oven.

Black Pepper and Garlic Chicken Wings

Editor's Note

Pawlcyn attributes the rich, deep flavor of this recipe to soy sauce that has been infused with mushrooms (called mushroom soy sauce). She uses this marinade for roast chicken and turkey, too. Mushroom soy sauce can be found in Asian markets, or you can use regular soy sauce as a substitute.

These are so-o-o delicious, and so-o-o easy to make! They are also very sticky, so be sure to have plenty of moist finger towels on hand when you serve them.

Instead of roasting these wings you could grill them over a medium-low to medium fire, but I find they get crisper in the oven. Remember to allow at least twelve hours to marinate the wings. It may seem like there's too much garlic and pepper in the recipe, but be brave—use it all.

SERVES 6

- ½ cup mushroom soy sauce
- 2 tablespoons brown sugar or palm sugar
- 1 tablespoon honey
- 2 tablespoons minced garlic
- 2 tablespoons freshly ground black pepper
- 3 pounds chicken wings

Minced garlic, chives, or scallions, for garnish

Combine the mushroom soy sauce, brown sugar, honey, garlic and black pepper in a bowl and mix the marinade well.

To prepare the wings, trim off and discard the tips, and cut each wing at the joint so you end up with one tiny drumstick and one flat section per wing. Place the wings in a sealable plastic bag or a large flat plastic container and pour the marinade over the wings, making sure that all surfaces are coated well. Close the bag tightly, and marinate in the refrigerator for 12 to 24 hours, shaking or turning the wings often.

To cook the wings, preheat the oven to 450°F. Arrange the wings on a rack in a shallow roasting pan. Roast for 12 to 18 minutes, until the skin is dark brown and crispy and the meat has begun to shrink away from the ends of the bones. The juices should run clear when the wings are pierced with a knife point. Sprinkle with the garnishes and serve them up!

best of the best exclusive

Spanish-Style Tuna Melts

4 SERVINGS

  2 tablespoons salted roasted almonds

Three 6-ounce cans tuna packed in water, drained

  ¼ cup mayonnaise

  ¼ cup minced onion

  ¼ cup pimiento-stuffed green olives, coarsely chopped

  3 piquillo peppers, cut into ¼-inch dice

  1 tablespoon chopped flat-leaf parsley

  1 small garlic clove, minced

  1 tablespoon sherry vinegar

Kosher salt and freshly ground pepper

Four ½-inch-thick slices of rustic white bread cut from a round loaf

  8 thin slices of Manchego cheese (2 ounces)

  8 thin slices of sharp white cheddar cheese (2 ounces)

1. Preheat the oven to 350°. Spread the almonds in a pie plate and toast for about 6 minutes, until fragrant. Let cool slightly, then coarsely chop. Turn the broiler on.

2. In a medium bowl, mix the tuna with the mayonnaise, onion, olives, piquillo peppers, parsley, garlic, sherry vinegar and chopped almonds. Season with salt and pepper.

3. Lay the bread slices on a baking sheet and broil 3 inches from the heat for about 2 minutes, turning once, until browned around the edges. Spoon the tuna over the toasts and top each sandwich with 2 slices each of the Manchego and cheddar cheeses. Broil the sandwiches for 1 more minute, or until the cheese is bubbly. Serve hot.

Editor's Note

Pawlcyn serves these tuna melts at her seafood-focused restaurant, Go Fish. She adds smoky piquillo peppers—a tapas favorite—along with roasted almonds, green olives, sherry vinegar and Manchego cheese to give the melt a Spanish twist.

A well-stocked kitchen helps put anyone in the mood for cooking.

The Good Home Cookbook

Edited by Richard J. Perry

This collection of more than 1,000 classic American dishes is an ode to home cooking in more ways than one. Not only did former chef Richard Perry cull the recipes from hundreds of vintage cookbooks, many from his own collection, but he enlisted 700 home cooks to help test his discoveries. He and his team corresponded regularly until each recipe was perfect. The result is an idiosyncratic compendium of all-American dishes, including immigrant-inspired ones such as a fresh, spicy Chicken Chili Verde and an eggy German Pancake.

Published by Collectors Press, $29.95.

German Pancake

Perry on Pancake Perfection

This recipe is based on one I learned in home ec class; it's the first dish I ever cooked for my mom. A cast-iron skillet will give you the best results. The higher gluten content of bread flour helps the batter rise; while all-purpose flour can be substituted, the results won't be as dramatic. Any type of apple is fine, but I love to offset the sugar with tart Granny Smiths.

SERVES 4

7 tablespoons butter, softened

2 large apples, peeled, cored, and sliced

2 tablespoons sugar

½ teaspoon ground cinnamon

6 large eggs, at room temperature

1 cup milk, at room temperature

1 cup bread flour

¼ teaspoon vanilla extract

Confectioners' sugar, to serve

1. Preheat the oven to 450°F. Place a large ovenproof skillet in the oven to preheat.

2. Melt 1 tablespoon of butter in a medium skillet over medium heat. Add the apples and sauté until softened, about 5 minutes. Stir in the sugar and ¼ teaspoon of cinnamon and heat until the sugar is melted. Remove the skillet from the heat and set aside.

3. In a large bowl, beat the eggs with an electric mixer until light and frothy. Add the milk, flour, vanilla extract, and remaining ¼ teaspoon cinnamon. Beat for 5 minutes more. The batter will be thin but smooth and creamy.

4. Remove the hot skillet from the oven. Add the remaining 6 tablespoons butter, tilting the pan to melt the butter and coat the skillet. Pour the batter into the hot skillet all at once, and immediately place the skillet in the oven.

5. Bake for 15 to 20 minutes, until the pancake is puffed and golden brown on top.

6. Remove the pancake from the oven, bringing it to the table in its pan or sliding it onto a serving plate. Once out of the oven, the pancake will begin to deflate. Dust it with confectioners' sugar, cut it into wedges, and transfer the wedges to individual plates. Top the wedges with the apple mixture and serve immediately.

The Good Home
Cookbook
Edited by Richard J. Perry

Chicken Chili Verde

SERVES 6

1½ pounds boneless, skinless chicken thighs, cut into ½-inch pieces

Salt and pepper

 3 tablespoons all-purpose flour

¼ cup oil

 2 medium onions, chopped

 1 tablespoon minced garlic

¾ cup seeded and chopped Anaheim or jalapeño chile peppers

 1 medium green bell pepper, seeded and cut lengthwise into ¼-inch strips

2½ cups frozen corn, thawed

 3 cups chicken broth (recipe follows)

 6 tomatillos, husked and coarsely chopped

 1 tablespoon chili powder

1½ teaspoons ground cumin

1½ teaspoons ground oregano

½ teaspoon paprika

 1 cinnamon stick

½ cup chopped fresh cilantro

Tortilla chips, to serve

1. Sprinkle the chicken with salt and pepper. Toss with the flour in a bowl.

2. Heat 1 tablespoon of oil in a large skillet over medium-high heat. Add the chicken and sauté until golden brown, about 10 minutes. Transfer to a large saucepan.

3. Heat 1 tablespoon of oil in the same skillet over medium-high heat. Add the onions and garlic and sauté until the onions are softened, about 3 minutes. Transfer to the pan with the chicken.

4. Heat 1 tablespoon of oil in the same skillet over medium-high heat. Add the chile peppers and bell pepper. Sauté until tender, about 4 minutes. Transfer to the pan with the chicken.

Perry on Toppings

Sour cream is the classic topping for this chili, and its smooth texture and tangy flavor work really well here. You can also pass around a bottle of hot sauce for anyone who likes extra spice.

5. Heat the remaining 1 tablespoon of oil in the same skillet. Sauté the corn until tender, about 2 minutes. Transfer to the pan with the chicken.

6. Add the broth, tomatillos, chili powder, cumin, oregano, paprika, and cinnamon stick to the pan with the chicken. Bring to a boil. Reduce the heat and simmer until the mixture thickens for about 1 hour or to your liking.

7. Remove the cinnamon stick and stir in the cilantro. Serve hot, passing the tortilla chips at the table.

Chicken Broth

MAKES 2 TO 3 QUARTS, PLUS ABOUT 8 CUPS COOKED CHICKEN

- 3 to 4 pounds chicken parts
- 1 large onion, quartered
- 4 medium celery ribs, chopped
- 4 garlic cloves
- 1 bunch fresh parsley
- 4 quarts water

Salt (optional)

1. Combine the chicken, onion, celery, garlic, and parsley in a large soup pot or saucepan. Add the water. Cover and bring just to a boil. Immediately reduce the heat and simmer gently for 2 hours with the lid partially on. Season to taste with salt, if using.

2. Strain into a clean pot and discard the vegetables. Remove the meat from the bones.

3. Refrigerate or freeze the meat. Chill the broth for several hours. Skim off and discard the fat that rises to the surface and hardens. Use the broth immediately or cover and refrigerate. The broth and meat will keep for about 3 days in the refrigerator or 4 to 5 months in the freezer.

Best Berry Muffins

You can substitute any berry you have on hand for these delicious muffins. This recipe adds a cinnamon-sugar topping to match the lightly spiced berry batter. You don't have to defrost berries before adding them to muffin batter.

MAKES 12

TOPPING

¼ cup all-purpose flour

2 tablespoons packed brown sugar

¼ teaspoon ground cinnamon

2 tablespoons butter, softened

MUFFINS

2 cups all-purpose flour

2 teaspoons baking powder

½ teaspoon salt

¼ teaspoon ground cinnamon

½ cup (1 stick) butter, softened

½ cup sugar

1 large egg

¾ cup milk

½ teaspoon vanilla extract

½ cup fresh or frozen blueberries

½ cup fresh or frozen raspberries

1. Preheat the oven to 400°F. Grease and flour a 12-cup muffin pan or line the pan with paper baking cups.

2. To make the topping, combine the flour, brown sugar, and cinnamon in a small bowl. Mix in the butter with a fork or pastry blender until the mixture is crumbly. Set aside.

3. To make the muffins, stir together the flour, baking powder, salt, and cinnamon in a medium bowl. Set aside.

Editor's Note

This batter makes a delicious, all-purpose muffin. Berries are great in it, but you can also use chopped apple, nuts, sliced banana, chocolate chips, or citrus zest.

4. Beat the butter and sugar in a medium bowl until light and fluffy. Beat in the egg, milk, and vanilla extract. Add the flour mixture and stir just until moistened. Fold in the berries.

5. Divide the batter evenly among the muffin cups. Sprinkle each with the topping.

6. Bake for 25 to 30 minutes or until golden brown.

7. Cool for 10 minutes, remove from the pan, and cool briefly on wire racks. Serve warm or cooled.

best of the best exclusive
Cucumber-Dill Deviled Eggs

6 SERVINGS

  8 large eggs

  3 tablespoons plain whole-milk yogurt

  1 teaspoon finely chopped dill

⅛ teaspoon garlic powder

Pinch of cayenne pepper

⅓ cup peeled, seeded and finely diced English cucumber,
     plus 8 thin, unpeeled cucumber slices, halved

Kosher salt and freshly ground black pepper

1. Bring a large saucepan of water to a boil. Gently add the eggs and cook for 12 minutes. Drain the eggs and immediately cool them under cold running water. Add ice cubes to the saucepan and let the eggs stand until completely cool.

2. Drain and peel the eggs. Halve the eggs lengthwise and gently remove the yolks. Transfer 6 yolks to a medium bowl; reserve the remaining 2 yolks for another use. Lightly mash the yolks in the bowl with a fork. Stir in the yogurt, dill, garlic powder and cayenne. Gently fold in the diced cucumber and season with salt and black pepper.

3. Arrange the egg white halves on a platter and fill the cavities with the yolk mixture. Top each deviled egg with a cucumber slice and serve.

MAKE AHEAD The assembled deviled eggs can be refrigerated overnight.

Editor's Note

These addictive deviled eggs have a nice crunch in the filling that comes from diced cucumber. This recipe is one of many variations from Perry's next book, *Deviled Eggcetera*.

That Chocolate Cake, p. 200

The Essence of Chocolate

By John Scharffenberger & Robert Steinberg

Since John Scharffenberger and Robert Steinberg founded Scharffen Berger over a decade ago, the brand has become synonymous with premium chocolate. Now the pair has compiled more than 100 recipes from their favorite chef friends to showcase their chocolates. Organized by cocoa quantity (Intensely Chocolate, A Hint of Chocolate), the recipes are interspersed with erudite essays on how Scharffen Berger sources and creates its chocolate. It's the perfect introduction to the ingredient, and one of our favorite dessert cookbooks of the year.

With Ann Krueger Spivack and Susie Heller; published by Hyperion, $35.

That Chocolate Cake

If you could only have one recipe for chocolate cake, this would be the one. It's the quintessential chocolate cake with chocolate frosting, rich and moist, completely satisfying, glorious without being the least bit formal. The best recipes are passed along, gaining fans each time they're given to somebody new, and this one was given to Susie Heller by her friend Jackie, who was given the recipe by a different Susie, who got the recipe from a chef in the Caribbean. Grown-ups love it, kids love it. This one is hard to beat.

SERVES 8 TO 10

FROSTING

1¼ cups granulated sugar

  1 cup heavy cream

  5 ounces 99% unsweetened chocolate, finely chopped

  8 tablespoons (4 ounces) unsalted butter, cut into ½-inch pieces

  1 teaspoon pure vanilla extract

CAKE

Unsalted butter and flour for the pans

  2 cups granulated sugar

1¾ cups all-purpose flour

 ¾ cup unsweetened cocoa powder

  1 teaspoon salt

1½ teaspoons baking powder

1½ teaspoons baking soda

  2 large eggs, lightly beaten

 ½ cup canola oil

  1 cup whole milk

  1 cup boiling water

FOR THE FROSTING:

In a small saucepan, combine the sugar and cream and bring to a boil over medium heat, stirring occasionally. Reduce the heat and simmer for 6 minutes. Add the chocolate and butter and stir until melted. Pour into a bowl and stir in the vanilla.

Let the frosting cool, whisking gently from time to time. Don't overwhip, or you'll create air bubbles.

FOR THE CAKE:

Position a rack in the center of the oven and preheat to 350°F. Lightly butter the bottom of two 9-inch round cake pans. Line the bottom with parchment paper, then butter and flour the parchment and the sides of the pans.

In the bowl of a stand mixer fitted with the paddle attachment, combine the sugar, flour, cocoa, salt, baking powder, and baking soda, mixing on low speed. Mix in the eggs, oil, and milk.

Increase the speed to medium and beat for 2 minutes. Reduce the speed to low and mix in the water. The batter will be soupy.

Divide the batter evenly between the cake pans. Bake for 30 to 35 minutes, or until a skewer inserted in the center comes out clean.

Remove from the oven and cool on a cooling rack for 5 minutes, then turn the layers out onto the rack and cool completely.

When the cakes have cooled, check the frosting. It should have the consistency of mayonnaise. If it is still too thin, allow it to cool longer.

TO FROST THE CAKE:

Place one cake layer on a serving plate. Spread the frosting with a hot palette knife or icing spatula to give the frosting a beautiful shine: Run the knife under hot tap water and dry with a towel. Spread about ¾ cup of the frosting over the top of the first layer. Top with the second layer. Spread the remaining frosting over the top and sides of the cake, heating the knife again as necessary.

Editor's Note

The time it takes for the frosting to reach a thick, mousselike consistency will depend on the temperature in your kitchen. Leave a couple hours of leeway if it's a warm day, or pop the frosting into the fridge very briefly, stirring every few minutes, until it has thickened—but take care not to chill it for too long or the frosting can get too thick to spread well.

Chocolate Mousse

Few people are as passionate about chocolate as David Lebovitz, who contributed this recipe. His recipes reflect both his years of experience in the pastry department at Chez Panisse and his great skill as a teacher— they're straightforward and produce impressive results. David says, "Forget light and ethereal. A real chocolate mousse should be thick and rich." Its richness comes not from uncooked eggs but from a silky custard base.

You can pour the mousse mixture into goblets, but David prefers to refrigerate it in a single large bowl. To serve, he scoops the mousse into individual glasses on top of a light layer of whipped cream.

SERVES 6

12 ounces 70% bittersweet chocolate, finely chopped

 4 large egg yolks

 1 cup whole milk

 3 tablespoons granulated sugar

⅔ cup heavy cream

Whipped Cream (recipe follows)

Chocolate shavings, cacao nibs, or cocoa powder, for garnish (optional)

Place a medium bowl and a whisk in the refrigerator or freezer to chill.

Place the chocolate in a large bowl, and set a fine-mesh strainer over the bowl.

In a medium bowl, stir together the egg yolks.

In a medium saucepan, bring the milk and 2 tablespoons of the sugar to a simmer, stirring until the sugar has dissolved. Slowly pour the milk into the egg yolks, stirring constantly with a heatproof rubber spatula or wooden spoon. Pour the mixture back into the saucepan and cook, stirring constantly, over medium heat for 6 to 10 minutes, or until it is thick enough to coat the back of a wooden spoon. Remove from the heat and strain the custard onto the chocolate. Stir gently until the chocolate has melted completely. Let cool to room temperature.

In the chilled bowl with the chilled whisk, whip the cream until it holds soft peaks. Whip in the remaining 1 tablespoon sugar and whip just until the cream holds a shape. Do not overwhip, or the mousse may be grainy.

Fold the whipped cream into the chocolate mixture. Cover with plastic wrap and refrigerate for 4 hours, or until set.

To serve, place a dollop of whipped cream in the bottom of each goblet or bowl. Dip an ice cream scoop in hot water, dry it, and scoop the mousse onto the cream. Garnish with a sprinkling of shaved chocolate, cacao nibs, or cocoa powder.

Whipped Cream

A cold bowl and whisk will give you much better results when you whip cream. Chill the bowl, the whisk or whisk attachment, and the cream until very cold.

MAKES 2 CUPS

- 1 **cup very cold heavy cream**
- 1 **tablespoon plus 2 teaspoons granulated sugar**

Place the cream in a chilled metal bowl or mixer bowl. With a whisk, or the whisk attachment, whip the cream until slightly frothy. Sprinkle in the sugar and continue to whip until soft peaks form. Use immediately, or refrigerate for up to 1 hour.

TO MAKE COCOA WHIPPED CREAM:

Combine the sugar with 1 tablespoon plus 1 teaspoon unsweetened cocoa powder before adding it to the cream.

Banana Caramel Cake

We tasted many recipes combining chocolate and bananas before choosing this one, which is basically a chocolate and banana cake with caramel poured over just as it comes from the oven. Don't give in to the temptation to add extra bananas to the mix, or the cake will acquire a gummy texture. The creamy bananas and the caramel layer keep this flavorful cake moist for days.

SERVES 12

CAKE

Unsalted butter and flour for the pan

- 3 cups sifted all-purpose flour
- ½ teaspoon ground cinnamon
- ¼ teaspoon freshly grated nutmeg
- ¼ teaspoon ground cloves
- 1 teaspoon salt
- 1 teaspoon baking soda
- 3 large eggs, lightly beaten
- 1¼ cups canola oil
- 2 cups granulated sugar
- 1 teaspoon pure vanilla extract
- ½ teaspoon pure almond extract
- ½ cup coarsely chopped toasted pecans
- 3 ounces 62% semisweet chocolate, chopped into chip-size chunks
- 1½ cups diced (¼-inch) ripe bananas (about 2 bananas)

CARAMEL

- ½ cup firmly packed light brown sugar
- 2 tablespoons whole milk
- 4 tablespoons (2 ounces) unsalted butter, cut into chunks

Editor's Note

This cake is also great plain if you want to leave out the caramel topping. Semisweet chips from the supermarket are fine for this recipe, although top-notch chocolate will make it that much better.

Banana Caramel Cake

Position a rack in the middle of the oven and preheat the oven to 350°F. Butter and flour a 12-cup (10-inch) nonstick Bundt pan.

In a medium bowl, combine the flour, cinnamon, nutmeg, cloves, salt, and baking soda.

In the bowl of a stand mixer fitted with the paddle attachment, combine the eggs, oil, granulated sugar, vanilla, and almond extract. Mix on medium speed until thoroughly combined, stopping to scrape the sides of the bowl as necessary. Mix in the dry ingredients, about ½ cup at a time, stopping to scrape the bowl as necessary.

Remove the bowl from the mixer and fold in the pecans and the chocolate. Carefully fold in the bananas; do not overmix.

Pour into the prepared pan. Bake for 50 minutes to 1 hour, or until a skewer inserted in the center of the cake comes out clean.

Meanwhile, about 5 minutes before the cake is done, combine the brown sugar, milk, and butter in a small saucepan and bring to a boil over medium heat, swirling the pan occasionally as the butter and sugar melt. Once it is amber in color, remove from the heat.

Remove the cake from the oven and immediately, using a long skewer, poke holes all over the surface of the cake. Pour the hot caramel over the top, poking more holes and pushing the cake slightly away from the sides of the pan as necessary to allow the caramel to soak into the cake's top and sides. Place on a cooling rack to cool slightly.

When the cake has cooled, but is still warm to the touch, unmold onto a serving platter.

Serve warm or at room temperature.

Pull-Apart Kuchen

Editor's Note

This is a great recipe for brunch or breakfast, and it's excellent for a buffet. Try to time the baking so that the kuchen is still warm from the oven when you serve it— that's when it's at its best.

Also known as monkey bread, this version of kuchen lets you roll balls of dough in ground pecans and semisweet chocolate. When the kuchen is hot out of the oven, it takes some restraint to wait for it to cool long enough to avoid burning your fingers.

SERVES 8

DOUGH

¼ cup warm water (110° to 115°F)

2½ teaspoons active dry yeast

3 large egg yolks, lightly beaten

8 tablespoons (4 ounces) unsalted butter

1 cup whole milk

¼ teaspoon salt

⅓ cup granulated sugar

4 cups all-purpose flour

TOPPING

¾ cup coarsely chopped toasted pecans (about 2½ ounces)

¾ cup coarsely chopped 62% semisweet chocolate (about 4 ounces)

½ cup granulated sugar

8 tablespoons (4 ounces) unsalted butter, melted

Butter and sugar for the pan

FOR THE DOUGH:

In a small bowl, combine the water and yeast and stir to dissolve. Let stand for 10 minutes or until foamy.

Place the yolks in the bowl of a stand mixer fitted with the paddle attachment. In a small saucepan, heat the butter and milk over medium-low heat until the butter has melted. With the mixer running on low speed, carefully pour the butter mixture into the yolks, and mix until combined. Let stand until just warm to the touch.

With the mixer on low speed, add the salt, sugar, and yeast mixture, mixing until just combined. Stop the mixer and add 2 cups of the flour, then mix on low speed until just incorporated. There will still be some lumps. Add the remaining 2 cups flour and mix for 30 seconds. Increase the speed to medium and continue to mix until the dough is smooth, about 5 minutes; it will still be sticky.

Lightly butter a large bowl. Using a plastic dough scraper, transfer the dough to the bowl. Turn to coat the dough with butter. Cover with a kitchen towel or plastic wrap and let rise in a warm place for 1 to 1½ hours, or until doubled in size.

FOR THE TOPPING:

Place the pecans, chocolate, and sugar in a food processor and pulse until the mixture has a sandy consistency. Set aside. Butter and sugar a 12-cup (10-inch) Bundt pan.

Pour the melted butter into a small bowl. Pull off small pieces of the dough, and roll into balls about the size of a golf ball. Roll in the butter, then in the nut and chocolate mixture to coat, and place in the prepared pan. Line the bottom of the pan and then stack more coated balls on top until all of the dough is used. Arrange the balls (and make smaller balls if necessary) so that the top layer is fairly even. Cover with a kitchen towel or plastic wrap and let rise in a warm spot for about 1 hour, or until doubled in size. Reserve any remaining melted butter.

Position a rack in the middle of the oven and preheat the oven to 350°F. Brush the top of the kuchen with any remaining melted butter. Bake for 45 to 50 minutes, or until the top is dark brown and a skewer inserted in the center comes out clean. The melted chocolate and sugar will be hot, so be careful.

Let the kuchen stand for 3 to 5 minutes, then turn out onto a cooling rack and let cool for 15 minutes. Serve warm.

best of the best exclusive

Cacao-Dusted Butternut Squash Soup

6 TO 8 SERVINGS

- 1 tablespoon unsalted butter
- 2 tablespoons extra-virgin olive oil
- 2 large leeks, white and tender green parts only, thinly sliced
- 1 medium butternut squash (2½ pounds)—peeled, seeded and cut into 2-inch pieces
- 1 baking potato, peeled and cut into 2-inch pieces
- 6 cups chicken stock or low-sodium broth
- 1 teaspoon fresh lemon juice

Kosher salt and freshly ground pepper

- 1 teaspoon cacao nibs (optional), finely ground (see Note)

1. In a large soup pot, melt the butter in the olive oil. Add the leeks and cook over moderately low heat, stirring occasionally, until very tender, about 15 minutes. Add the squash, potato and stock and bring to a boil. Cover and simmer over moderate heat until the squash and potato are very tender, about 40 minutes.

2. Working in batches, puree the soup in a blender until smooth. Return it to the soup pot and rewarm. Stir in the lemon juice and season with salt and pepper. Ladle the soup into bowls, sprinkle with the ground cacao nibs and serve.

NOTE Cacao nibs are roasted pieces of cocoa bean that have been separated from their husks and broken into small pieces. They're available at specialty markets or at scharffenberger.com.

MAKE AHEAD The soup can be made up to 3 days in advance and refrigerated. Rewarm before serving.

Editor's Note

This is Robert Steinberg's version of a sweet pumpkin soup he had in France. He tops his with cacao nibs, which have an earthy scent that contrasts well with the sweetness of the squash. Grinding releases their aroma: Pulse the cacao nibs in a mini food processor or spice grinder. Alternately, crush the nibs with a mortar and pestle into a fine powder.

Chipotle Grilled Chicken with
Avocado Salsa, p. 214

¡Baja! Cooking on the Edge

By Deborah M. Schneider

Deborah Schneider's cookbook is testament to her decades-long love affair with Baja California, the skinny peninsula off the west coast of Mexico. Physically isolated from the rest of the country, the region has a distinct style of cooking that might be best described as a lighter version of Mexican food, influenced by its American neighbors and made with plenty of seafood, produce and chiles. Schneider's recipes, gleaned from watching cooks at roadside stands and local markets, are also fast and easy to make.

Published by Rodale, Inc., $27.95.

Chipotle Grilled Chicken with Avocado Salsa

Editor's Note

We found that adding a little extra salt to this recipe really heightened the flavors in the dish. For the best results, give the chicken pieces a generous sprinkle of salt just before grilling.

Juicy roasters get a smoky, spicy kick from chipotles in adobo, which contrast beautifully with the creamy coolness of the avocado salsa. If you have no grill, roast the chickens in the oven.

MAKES 6 SERVINGS

- 1 can (7 ounces) chipotles in adobo
- 4 large garlic cloves
- 2 tablespoons vegetable oil
- 1 teaspoon kosher salt
- 3 small whole chickens, cut into halves or quarters

TO SERVE

Fresh corn tortillas, warmed

Avocado Salsa (recipe follows)

1. In a food processor, puree the chipotles, garlic, oil, and salt. Wipe the chickens with paper towels. Thoroughly coat the pieces on all sides with a layer of the chipotle paste.

2. Place in a nonreactive baking dish or in resealable bags and refrigerate for 2 hours, or as long as overnight.

3. Heat the grill to medium. With the lid open, grill the chicken on both sides until well marked but not burned—about 7 minutes per side. Turn the heat to low, close the lid, and cook the chicken, skin side up, until an instant-read thermometer inserted in the thickest part of the thigh reads 165 degrees. (Alternatively, bake at 350 degrees for approximately 30 to 40 minutes.)

4. Serve with the tortillas and salsa.

Avocado Salsa

This is not guacamole but chunks of buttery Hass avocado mixed with raw onion and cilantro—more like an avocado salad. The best avocados come from Southern California and Mexico, and the tastiest variety is the Hass. They are small, with pebbly black skins and smooth, rich flesh.

MAKES 1½ CUPS

3 ripe Hass avocados, pitted, peeled, and cut into ½-inch pieces

Kosher salt

Juice of 1 lime, preferably a Mexican limón (see Limones)

⅓ cup finely diced white onion

3 cilantro sprigs, stemmed and chopped

Place the avocados in a bowl. Sprinkle with the salt and lime juice; mix gently with the onion and cilantro (don't mash; it should look diced).

NOTE The Avocado Salsa should be served within 3 hours. To hold longer, press a piece of plastic wrap directly onto the surface of the salsa and refrigerate until needed.

LIMONES Mexican limes (*limones*) are small, with thin skin that is mottled green and yellow when ripe. One little lime produces a copious amount of juice, far sweeter and more fragrant than the limes found in American supermarkets, which tend to be bitter and dry. It is worth seeking out a Latin market just to buy decent limes. They are used in almost everything in Baja.

Schneider on Tortillas

I always use corn rather than flour tortillas, and I buy them right from a *tortillaria* (fresh tortilla maker) whenever I can. To warm them, heat a nonstick pan until fairly hot but not scorching. Press the tortilla down onto it briefly, turn and press again; it will become soft and flexible. Transfer immediately to a clean towel or tortilla warmer.

Chipotle Crab Cakes with Tamarind Sauce

Serve these as an appetizer topped with the tart-sweet tamarind sauce and buttery-rich avocado—or the salsa of your choice. Bite-size versions are great with cocktails.

MAKES ABOUT 20 APPETIZER OR 30 COCKTAIL CRAB CAKES

 1 pound Dungeness crabmeat, picked over

¼ white onion, minced

 1 celery stalk, finely minced

¼ medium red bell pepper, minced

¼ cup packed cilantro leaves, finely chopped

Juice of 1 lemon

 2 teaspoons kosher salt

¼ cup mayonnaise

 2 eggs, beaten

 2 tablespoons pureed chipotle chiles

1 to 1½ cups homemade bread crumbs, dried out

Panko bread crumbs (available in Asian markets)

Oil, for shallow frying

TO SERVE

Tamarind Sauce (recipe follows)

Diced avocado

1. In a bowl, combine the crab, onion, celery, bell pepper, cilantro, lemon juice, and salt.

2. Place the mixture in a colander or sieve set inside a bowl. Set a plate on the crab, weight with a can, cover, and refrigerate for 12 to 24 hours to drain.

3. Transfer the crab to a bowl and stir in the mayonnaise, eggs, and chipotles. Add ¾ cup of the bread crumbs and toss to combine. The mixture should look moist (not gummy) and should stick together without crumbling. You may need to add more bread crumbs, little by little, to achieve the desired texture.

Schneider on Crab

Not only is wild Dungeness crab delicious, it's also a sustainable American seafood. Alaska king crab is another sustainable— if more expensive—choice that would be great here.

4. Spread a generous layer of panko on a plate. Scoop out balls of the crab mixture, using ¼ cup for appetizers or 1½ tablespoons for cocktail servings. Drop the balls into the panko. Roll around to coat and press gently into thick patties. Shake off excess crumbs. (The crab cakes may be made to this point and refrigerated.)

5. Heat a 12-inch nonstick skillet over medium-low heat. Add enough oil to generously cover the bottom of the pan ⅛ inch deep (about ¼ cup). Cook the crab cakes until crisp and golden brown on both sides and firm. Drain and keep warm. Serve with a little tamarind sauce on the plate and some diced avocado.

Tamarind Sauce

MAKES 1½ CUPS

½ cup tamarind paste

¾ cup boiling water

 2 to 3 tablespoons cold water

 2 teaspoons brown sugar

½ teaspoon freshly squeezed lime juice,
    preferably from a Mexican limón (see Limones, page 215)

¼ teaspoon kosher salt

 1 tablespoon butter

1. Break the tamarind paste into pieces in a small heatproof bowl. Pour on the boiling water, stir to combine, and soak for 30 minutes. Rub the paste through a coarse sieve to remove the seeds and fibrous strands. You should have about ¼ cup of tamarind mixture.

2. In a small saucepan, combine the tamarind puree, cold water, brown sugar, lime juice, and salt. Warm over gentle heat; do not boil. Whisk in the butter and keep the sauce warm until needed.

Fresh Corn Strata with Crispy Onions and Oven-Roasted Tomatoes

I never tire of playing with the subtle and sweet flavor of fresh white corn, which here features a savory take on another home-style Mexican favorite: bread pudding (*capirotada*). Leftover bread and silky corn custard are combined with layers (strata) of cheese and baked until firm and creamy. Crispy onions and slow-cooked tomatoes add color and crunch.

The strata may be made the day before and baked before serving, which makes it ideal for brunch or buffet.

MAKES 6 TO 8 GENEROUS SERVINGS

- 3 ears sweet white corn
- 1 tablespoon vegetable oil
- ½ medium white onion, diced
- 2 cups water
- ¼ teaspoon baking soda
- 1½ teaspoons kosher salt
- 2 cups milk or 1 cup milk and 1 cup cream
- ½ teaspoon freshly ground black pepper
- ⅛ teaspoon freshly ground nutmeg
- ½ teaspoon cayenne pepper
- 4 eggs
- 1 tablespoon butter, softened
- 1 loaf (1 pound) firm white bread, crusts removed
- 2 cups grated Menonito, Chihuahua, or Jack cheese

Oven-Roasted Tomatoes and Garlic (recipe follows)

ONIONS

- ½ cup vegetable oil
- ⅓ cup all-purpose flour

Kosher salt and freshly ground black pepper

- ½ white onion, cut into ¼-inch slices

Schneider on Mexican Cheeses

Both Chihuahua and Menonito cheese come from the Mexican state of Chihuahua, which was settled by German Mennonites in the 19th century. These soft, mild cow's-milk cheeses are good for melting. They are less salty than most Mexican cheeses; and unlike most Mexican cheeses, which are made to be eaten right away, these are sometimes briefly aged.

Fresh Corn Strata with Crispy Onions
and Oven-Roasted Tomatoes

1. Trim the ends of the corn and stand on end on a plate. With a sharp knife, scrape all of the kernels from the cobs; this should yield about 3 cups. Be sure to catch any corn "milk." Cut the cobs in half and set aside.

2. Heat the oil over medium heat in a 2-quart saucepan. Add the onion and corn; cook, stirring often, until the onion is softened. Add the water, corn cobs, baking soda, and salt. Simmer for 30 minutes. (Add a small amount of water during cooking to maintain the level, if necessary.)

3. When the corn is cooked, discard the cobs. Drain the corn, reserving the cooking liquid. Place the cooking liquid and half of the corn in a blender. Add the milk, pepper, nutmeg, and cayenne; blend on high speed for about 2 minutes, or until silky smooth. Taste for seasoning and add more salt and other spices if necessary; the custard should be highly seasoned. Add the eggs and blend on high speed for 30 seconds. You should have about 6 cups of custard.

4. Butter a shallow 3-quart baking dish (8 by 11 inches). Cut the bread into 1½-inch cubes. Cover the bottom of the baking dish with one-third of the bread cubes. Scatter on one-third of the cheese and half of the reserved corn kernels. Add another layer of bread, cheese, and corn. Top with the remaining bread and cheese. Pour the corn custard evenly over the bread; the mixture will be very wet. Cover and refrigerate for at least 4 hours.

5. Preheat the oven to 350 degrees. Bake the strata for 1 hour and 15 minutes, or until browned, puffed in the center, and firm to the touch. Be careful not to overcook or the custard will curdle and break. During the last 5 minutes of baking, place the tomatoes in the oven to heat.

6. Make the onions while the strata is baking: Heat the oil in a small saucepan over medium-high heat. Combine the flour and pinches of salt and pepper in a small paper bag. Add the onions and shake to coat. Shake off any excess flour and fry the onions in batches until crisp and brown. Drain on paper towels.

7. Serve the strata warm, with the roasted tomatoes and a scattering of onions.

Oven-Roasted Tomatoes and Garlic

Slow-roasting intensifies the sweet/acid joy of good tomatoes and improves the flavor of not-so-great ones. Use fleshy tomatoes, such as Romas, and make a batch when you have the oven on for something else. They take about an hour to cook and keep well for several days. They're especially delicious warm from the oven, with garlic-rubbed toasted bread, olives, and a salty cheese. Gently rewarm any leftovers and use on salads or on grilled bread.

MAKES 24 HALF TOMATOES

12 ripe Roma or pear tomatoes

Kosher salt

½ teaspoon freshly ground or cracked black pepper

4 to 6 large garlic cloves

About ½ cup olive oil

Small rosemary sprig (optional)

1. Preheat the oven to 325 degrees.

2. Remove the tomato cores with the tip of a sharp knife and cut the tomatoes in half lengthwise. Scoop out the seeds and juice; turn upside down to drain for several minutes.

3. Season the tomatoes inside and out with the salt and pepper. Set hollow sides down on a rimmed cookie sheet with the garlic. Drizzle with several tablespoons of the oil and tuck in the rosemary sprig. Roast without stirring for about 1 hour, or until softened and shrunken.

4. Remove from the oven and cool; drizzle the pan juices over the tomatoes. Transfer to a small container and pour in the remaining oil and the pan juices. Cover, store in the refrigerator, and use within 3 days.

best of the best exclusive

Mushroom and Gorgonzola Tartlets

8 SERVINGS

- 2 tablespoons plus 2 teaspoons extra-virgin olive oil
- 1 pound mixed mushrooms, such as cremini, shiitake and oyster, stemmed and thinly sliced
- 1 teaspoon thyme leaves, coarsely chopped

Kosher salt and freshly ground pepper

All-purpose flour, for dusting

One 14-ounce package frozen puff pastry, thawed

- 1 small red onion, halved and thinly sliced
- ¼ pound Gorgonzola cheese, crumbled

1. Preheat the oven to 400°. In a large skillet, heat 2 tablespoons of the olive oil. Add the mushrooms and cook over moderately high heat, stirring occasionally, until golden around the edges, about 8 minutes. Stir in the thyme. Remove from the heat and season with salt and pepper.

2. On a lightly floured work surface, roll out the puff pastry ⅛ inch thick. Using a 4½ inch round biscuit cutter, stamp out 8 rounds. Transfer the pastry rounds to a large baking sheet. Prick them all over with a fork and freeze for 10 minutes.

3. In a small bowl, toss the onion with the remaining 2 teaspoons of olive oil. Sprinkle the Gorgonzola over the pastry rounds. Top with the sautéed mushrooms and the onion and season with pepper. Bake the tartlets for about 20 minutes, or until the bottoms and edges are browned. Serve hot or warm.

Editor's Note

Schneider says that any creamy cheese can be used in place of the Gorgonzola here—try a sharp blue or mild Jack if you prefer. She also suggests replacing some of the mushrooms with fresh cuitlacoche, a Mexican corn fungus often likened to truffles. Cuitlacoche can be found at Latin markets.

Chicken with Mushrooms
and Lemongrass, p. 226

The Kitchen Diaries

By Nigel Slater

London-based food columnist Nigel Slater feels passionate about eating seasonally. "Food [should be] eaten when the ingredients are at their peak perfection, when the food, the cook and the time of year are at one with each other," he writes in describing the philosophy behind his latest cookbook, a diary of his meals for a year. From a Thai lemongrass chicken bowl in March to a simple supper of orecchiette with juicy, just-ripe tomatoes on a warm summer's night, Slater provides pitch-perfect recipes for every season.

Published by Gotham Books, $40.
Find more recipes by Nigel Slater at foodandwine.com/slater

Chicken with Mushrooms and Lemongrass

Editor's Note

Field mushrooms are not very different from button mushrooms. In this recipe, a mix of wild and button mushrooms, or even just shiitake, will work nicely.

Hot, fast and refreshing, this is one of those knee-jerk bowls of food that I make when I have a bit of Thai stuff (lemongrass, limes, ginger and chile peppers) around. As instant suppers go, this is as good as it gets.

ENOUGH FOR 2

Garlic – 3 medium-sized cloves

Ginger – 4 slices

Scallions – 3

Lemongrass – 2 stalks

Peanut oil

Hot red chile peppers – 3

Diced chicken – ¾ pound

Field mushrooms – 3 medium-sized

Lime juice – 2 generous tablespoons

Nam pla (Thai fish sauce) – 2 generous tablespoons

Light brown or palm sugar – a teaspoon

A few leaves of Thai basil or mint

Peel and chop the garlic, shred the ginger, finely chop the scallions and very finely shred the tender inner leaves of the lemongrass.

Heat a couple of glugs of oil in a frying pan or wok. Add the garlic, ginger, scallions and lemongrass and let them sizzle over a moderately high heat till the garlic is golden. Halve the peppers, scrape out the seeds and discard them. Finely chop the flesh and add to the pan. Cook briefly, then tip the whole lot out into a bowl.

Get the pan really hot, pour in a little more oil and then add the chicken. Leave it to color, then stir and fry till the meat is golden brown and sticky on all sides. Cut the mushrooms into small segments and add them to the pan. When they are tender, return the aromatics to the pan. Mix the lime juice, *nam pla* and sugar in a cup, then pour this mixture into the hot pan. It will crackle and spit. Toss in the herb leaves and eat immediately.

Orecchiette with Roast Tomato and Basil Sauce

ENOUGH FOR 4 AS A MAIN DISH

Cherry or small tomatoes – 3 pounds

Garlic – 4 fat cloves

Olive oil

Dried orecchiette – 1 pound

Large basil leaves – 30

Heavy cream – 5 tablespoons

Grated Parmesan or pecorino cheese, to serve

Remove the stalks from the tomatoes and put the fruit into a small roasting pan. Peel the garlic and slice the cloves thinly, drop them in with the tomatoes and drizzle over a little olive oil. Put the tomatoes under the broiler and leave them until their skins are golden brown and black here and there and their insides are juicy and starting to burst. Don't pussyfoot around here; broil the tomatoes till their skins are truly blackened in some places. Meanwhile, cook the pasta in a deep saucepan of boiling, generously salted water.

Remove the tomatoes from the heat and crush them, skins and all, with a fork. Drop in the basil leaves and stir them in. They will wilt and soften with the heat of the fruit. Drain and add the cooked pasta. Stir in the cream, correct the seasoning with salt and coarsely ground black pepper, then eat straight away, with a spoon or two of grated Parmesan or pecorino.

Editor's Note

If you want to use another pasta instead of the orecchiette, choose a ridged shape with a twist or hole that will hold plenty of the creamy sauce.

Pumpkin and Tomato Laksa

Editor's Note

Cilantro roots are the green and pink base of the stems. If you can't find cilantro sold with its roots, use more stems in their place to make the spice paste for the laksa. When making the paste, you may need to drizzle in a little vegetable oil to help get it moving around the food processor bowl. (Note that this recipe uses only half the spice paste; the rest can be kept in the refrigerator for up to a week.)

ENOUGH FOR 4

Pumpkin – 9 ounces unpeeled weight

Small, red bird's eye chiles – 5

Garlic – 4 cloves

A lump of ginger the size of your thumb

Lemongrass – 2 plump stalks

Lime leaves – 6

Cilantro roots – 5 or 6, plus a large handful cilantro

Chicken or vegetable stock – 2 cups

Coconut milk – 1¾ cups

Cherry tomatoes – 24

Nam pla (Thai fish sauce) – 2 generous tablespoons

The juice of half a lemon

Dried noodles – ¼ pound, cooked as it says on the packet

Mint leaves – a large handful

Cut the pumpkin into large chunks and place in the top of a steamer. The pumpkin should be tender in 12 to 15 minutes. Remove from the heat.

Chop the chiles, removing the seeds first if you wish, peel the garlic and ginger and chop roughly. Put them all into a food processor. Discard the outer leaves of the lemongrass and roughly chop the inner leaves, shred the lime leaves, then add them to the chiles. Scrub the cilantro roots and add them to the chiles, along with half the cilantro leaves and stems. Process to a pulp.

Place a fairly deep pot over a moderate heat, add half the spice paste and fry it, moving it round the pot so it does not scorch. Do this for a minute or two, then pour in the stock and coconut milk and bring to a boil.

Cut the tomatoes in half and add them to the soup with the *nam pla* and lemon juice. They will take 7 to 10 minutes to cook. Add the pumpkin and continue cooking for a minute or two. Place a swirl of cooked noodles in each of 4 bowls, pour over the laksa and add the mint and the remaining cilantro.

Cannellini Beans with Coppa, Spinach and Mustard

Editor's Note

Coppa is an air-cured Italian pork sausage usually flavored with garlic and red wine. If it's not available, you can substitute hard salami or prosciutto.

ENOUGH FOR 2 AS A LIGHT LUNCH WITH BREAD

Dried cannellini beans – ¾ cup, soaked overnight in cold water

Small, tender spinach (or watercress) leaves – 4 handfuls

Thinly sliced coppa or other cured meat – 3 ounces

Basil leaves, the thicker and more pungent the better – a loose handful

FOR THE OLIVES

Extra-virgin olive oil – 6 tablespoons

Red wine vinegar – a generous tablespoon

Smooth Dijon mustard – a generous tablespoon

Fresh thyme leaves – a generous tablespoon, chopped

Black olives – 4 ounces

Drain the beans, then cook them to tenderness in a large, deep pot of unsalted boiling water. They will take anything from twenty-five to sixty minutes, depending on their age and size. They are ready as soon as you can easily crush them between finger and thumb.

Whilst the beans are cooking, mix the olive oil, vinegar and mustard with a fork in a small bowl, then whisk in the chopped thyme and some salt and pepper. The dressing will be thick and creamy. Pit the olives, dropping each one into the mustard dressing as you go. When the beans are ready, drain and toss them with the dressing. Set aside for an hour or so for the flavors to marry.

When you are ready to eat, rinse the spinach in cold water and shake it dry, removing all but the very finest stems. Put it into a large serving dish. Peel any shreds of skin from the outside of the coppa, then shred the meat into ribbons the width of thick matchsticks. Put them in with the spinach, separating the strips as you go. Tear the basil into small pieces, scattering it into the dish. Tip the beans, olives and dressing over, fold the ingredients gently together then serve.

Endive and Apple Salad with Grapes, Sumac, and Pecan Labne, p. 234

Spice

By Ana Sortun with Nicole Chaison

In her debut cookbook, Ana Sortun, the chef of Oleana restaurant in Cambridge, Massachusetts, uses the spices and herbs of the eastern Mediterranean to make deeply flavored dishes like her signature Crispy Lemon Chicken with Za'atar. "Spices create cravings," she says, explaining the inspiration for her recipes. Her cookbook is organized by complementary spices (for example, cumin, coriander and cardamom are placed together) and doubles as an excellent reference guide, with sources for hard-to-find spices and tips on storing them.

Published by Regan Books, $34.95.
Find more recipes by Ana Sortun at foodandwine.com/sortun

Endive and Apple Salad with Grapes, Sumac, and Pecan Labne

Editor's Note

Sumac is the ground berry of a bush that grows wild in the Middle East and parts of the Mediterranean (and is distantly related to poison sumac). Sortun says that sprinkling this bright-flavored, crimson dried spice on a dish "is like adding a squeeze of lemon." Sumac is available in Middle Eastern markets and at Penzeys Spices (penzeys.com).

This salad is timely in the fall or winter, when delicate, local, fresh greens disappear after the frost. Look for tight, juicy heads of endive.

Labne is simply yogurt cheese. Yogurt contains a lot of water, and when you strain the water off, the yogurt becomes thick like ricotta cheese. You can buy labne at most Middle Eastern grocery stores, or you can make it yourself by mixing Greek yogurt with a little salt to taste and straining it overnight in the refrigerator in a colander or sieve lined with cheesecloth. The key to making your own labne is using yogurt that is high in butterfat, so whole-milk yogurt works best. If you use low-fat yogurt, the cheese will have a chalky mouth feel that you can eliminate with a splash of heavy cream, replacing the fat that is needed.

This labne recipe is inspired by my friend Maria Hatziiliades, the best home cook I know. Maria and her husband Max are from Thessaloniki, and I met her while her husband was building the restaurant space for Oleana. Max and Maria have taught me much about Greek food: one year they invited me to Athens to attend their daughter's wedding, and they took me on a several-day whirlwind tour of Greek cuisine. Max also now serves as Oleana's olive oil and ouzo supplier, filling boat containers of organic olive oil and pure organic ouzo and shipping them directly from Greece to the restaurant. Maria made this pecan labne for dinner one night and served it with mastic bread, which is made with the resin from the bark of a mastic tree.

Sprinkle the sumac over the salad at the last minute to make the color stand out. If mixed in with the rest of the ingredients, sumac turns everything purple.

Pair this dish with an off-dry chenin blanc, such as a Vouvray, that marries well with the sweetness of the grapes and apples and the bitterness of the endive.

SERVES 6

1 cup pecan pieces

2 small crisp eating apples, such as Fuji or Granny Smith, unpeeled

1 tablespoon chopped fresh parsley

1 tablespoon chopped fresh mint

1 tablespoon chopped fresh dill

1 tablespoon freshly squeezed lemon juice

3 tablespoons extra-virgin olive oil

Salt and pepper to taste

1 small bunch red seedless grapes (about ½ pound), stemmed and washed

2 teaspoons finely chopped garlic (about 2 cloves)

1½ cups labne

3 tablespoons ground zwieback crackers or plain melba toast

3 heads endive

1 teaspoon sumac

1. Preheat the oven to 350°F.

2. Toast the pecan pieces on a heavy baking sheet for about 6 minutes, until they are fragrant. Cool for at least 10 minutes.

3. Core the apples and slice them in very thin rounds, about ⅛ inch thick. Julienne them by slicing across the rings into very skinny sticks. If you own a mandoline slicer, you can use the julienne blade.

4. Place the apples in a small mixing bowl and toss them with the parsley, mint, and dill and 2 teaspoons of the lemon juice and 1 tablespoon of the olive oil. Season them lightly with salt and pepper.

5. Cut the grapes in half, figuring 4 to 5 grapes per person, and add them to the apple mixture.

6. Place the garlic and the remaining 1 teaspoon of lemon juice in a small mixing bowl and let stand for 5 minutes to soften the raw garlic flavor.

7. Add the labne, the remaining 2 tablespoons of olive oil, the zwieback crumbs, and season with salt and pepper, and stir.

8. Finely chop the lightly toasted pecans by hand or in a food processor fitted with a metal blade. Reserve 1 tablespoon of the nuts for garnish and add the rest to the labne mixture.

9. Trim the bottom ends of the endive and remove the leaves, one by one. You will need to trim the bottom one more time to loosen the leaves. When you reach the heart or center of the endive and the leaves become very small and tight, set them aside.

10. Slice the endive hearts into thin rings and stir them into the apple mixture.

11. Assemble the salad by placing a quarter cup of labne on the bottom of each salad plate.

12. Using the back of a spoon, smooth the labne into a 2-inch circle. Arrange 5 endive spears on each plate, at a slight angle, sticking the bottom of the spears into the labne.

13. Spoon ½ tablespoon of the apple mixture over each endive spear. Sprinkle sumac and reserved pecan pieces over the salads and serve.

Creamy Parsnip Hummus with Parsley

Hummus versions abound, but most—except for some Turkish recipes—are made with chickpeas and tahini. Hummus means "chickpea" in Arabic, and it is taken very seriously in the Middle East, where people debate questions such as whether the chickpeas should be peeled before puréeing or whether chilling the tahini ruins its texture.

Sometimes I like to leave out the chickpeas and experiment with ingredients such as white beans, avocados, pumpkins, squash, and parsnips. This, of course, breaks the rules since technically hummus is not hummus without chickpeas. Oleana's customers, though, understand why I call this recipe hummus when they taste it. I purée parsnips in place of the chickpeas, but I flavor the dish with the traditional garlic, lemon, cumin, and tahini. The parsnip's texture is perfect for hummus: it is smooth and creamy, just like chickpeas, but has twice as much flavor.

In New England, parsnips are the first spring crop, even before spinach, nettles, or fiddleheads. Farmers like to harvest parsnips after they've "wintered over" because the freezing ground makes the sugars more intense. The sweetness of the parsnips paired with the bitter, nutty tahini and earthy cumin is just divine.

I happen to like the dramatic visual contrast of the white parsnip purée holding the dark tahini sauce, but if this presentation seems too fussy to you, you can combine the tahini with the parsnips before serving.

If you serve parsnip hummus as an hors d'oeuvre, try pairing it with a Falanghina from Italy; the flavors in the wine have just enough bitterness to set off the tahini and sweet parsnip.

Creamy Parsnip Hummus with Parsley (continued)

MAKES 4 CUPS TO SERVE 8 AS AN APPETIZER OR 4 AS PART OF A MEAL

- 1 pound parsnips (about 6 medium or 4 large), peeled and cut into 1-inch chunks
- 1 tablespoon chopped garlic (about 3 large cloves)
- ¼ cup freshly squeezed lemon juice
- 4 tablespoons butter, cut into small pieces
- ¼ cup extra-virgin olive oil
- 2 teaspoons ground cumin

Salt and pepper to taste

- ½ recipe tahini sauce (recipe follows)
- 2 tablespoons chopped fresh parsley

1. In a medium saucepan, cover the parsnips with water and bring them to a boil over high heat. Reduce the heat to medium and simmer the parsnips for about 20 minutes, until they are very tender when squeezed with a pair of tongs or pierced with a fork. Drain the parsnips in a colander, reserving 1 tablespoon of the cooking liquid or water.

2. Transfer the parsnips to the work bowl of a food processor fitted with a metal blade. Purée the parsnips with the reserved cooking liquid, garlic, lemon juice, butter, olive oil, and cumin until smooth and creamy, for about 3 minutes, stopping to scrape the sides of the bowl a couple of times.

3. Season the purée with salt and pepper. Spoon the purée into a serving bowl and cool it to room temperature, for about an hour.

4. Use the back of a large serving spoon to create a well in the center of the purée, big enough to hold about ½ cup. Spoon the tahini sauce into the center of the well. Garnish with parsley and serve.

Tahini Sauce

I prefer the dark-roasted variety of tahini from Tohum, available at www.tohum.com.

MAKES ½ CUP

¼ cup tahini

¼ cup extra-virgin olive oil

¾ teaspoon ground cumin

¾ teaspoon chopped garlic (about 1 clove)

1 teaspoon freshly squeezed lemon juice

Salt and pepper to taste

Place all the ingredients in a blender and blend until smooth. Season with salt and pepper. The tahini sauce will last for 3 to 5 days in the refrigerator.

Editor's Note

You'll only need half of the Tahini Sauce for the Parsnip Hummus, so halve this recipe or spoon the extra on salads, grilled lamb or roasted vegetables.

Crispy Lemon Chicken with Za'atar

Editor's Note

Za'atar, a wild herb that grows in the mountains along the eastern Mediterranean, tastes somewhat like a cross between thyme, oregano and summer savory. Za'atar also often refers to a seasoning that contains this herb, usually combined with sesame seeds, salt and sumac. Sortun prefers Jordanian blends, which she finds milder than Syrian and Lebanese versions. They're available at Middle Eastern markets and at Kalustyan's (kalustyans.com).

This is an Oleana favorite, and my customers would protest if I took it off the menu. I developed this recipe in my quest to find a chicken recipe that's interesting enough to make people want to order it from the menu or to prepare as a special meal at home.

In the United States, chicken is so mass-produced and inexpensive that we consider it to be a boring, everyday protein. And the flavor isn't terribly exciting either, unless you can find a free-range bird. A chicken that roams freely, eating grass, bugs, nuts, seeds, dark wild greens, herbs, and fallen tree fruits will taste a whole lot better than a chicken that has spent its life in a tiny cage. Natural and organic chickens—often fed grains to fatten them up quickly—are a good alternative if you can't find free-range. "Natural" means the birds haven't been treated with antibiotics or been given steroids. The same is true for organic chickens, and in addition, the feed these birds eat is certified organic.

Deboning and tucking butter and herbs into a chicken and then cooking it under a brick is a classic Tuscan preparation that makes the skin crispy and tight—not flabby or soggy. The brick presses the chicken down to an equal thickness throughout, so the meat cooks evenly and retains its moisture. At Oleana, we debone half a chicken intact, and tuck some of the dark thigh meat around the white breast, which marbles the chicken and enriches the flavor.

If you're daunted about deboning the chicken yourself, your butcher can do it for you. Or you can buy the pieces separately and serve the breast and thigh pieces side by side, as in the variation.

Don't be shy with the za'atar. Make sure you sprinkle each crispy chicken piece generously with this delicious spice mixture.

The chicken itself pairs wonderfully with a crisp, dry, snappy, and citrusy Assyrtiko from the Greek island of Santorini.

Crispy Lemon Chicken with Za'atar (continued)

Editor's Note

If you'd rather not use bricks to flatten the chicken parts, place a small, heatproof plate on each piece and weigh it down with a heavy can—or just wrap the can in foil and put it directly on the chicken.

SERVES 4

2 lemons, cut into ⅛-inch slices, seeds removed

¾ cup plus 1 tablespoon olive oil

7 tablespoons butter

Salt and pepper to taste

2 whole chickens, cut in half and deboned

2 terra-cotta bricks, like those found at a garden store, wrapped 3 times in aluminum foil

8 tablespoons za'atar (see Editor's Note, page 240)

1. Make the lemon confit. In a small saucepan over very low heat, cook the lemon slices in ¾ cup of the olive oil, slowly and gently (barely simmering) for about 1½ hours, or until soft and jamlike. Drain the oil off and discard because it tastes bitter. Cool for at least 10 minutes and then refrigerate for at least 20 minutes. The confit should be cool before you stuff the chicken; it can be made days ahead if kept covered in the refrigerator.

2. Cut the butter into 7 pieces and then into 14 pieces and then again into 28 pieces so that you have 28 small cubes.

3. Season the chicken with salt and pepper on all sides.

4. Create pockets under the chicken skin on both the thigh and breast with your fingers. Make the pockets as deep as you can without piercing all the way through to the other side.

5. Stuff 6 cubes of butter under the skin in each chicken half and then smear a tablespoon of lemon confit in the pockets. Press down on the skin so the butter and confit distribute evenly. The butter may spread only a little, and that's fine; the heat will melt it and the pressure from the bricks will force the butter to baste the meat as it cooks.

6. Place the chicken skin-side up and fold each half together, pressing the thigh meat up against the breast meat and forming a round shape.

7. In a large sauté pan (about 14 inches), heat 2 cubes of the leftover butter with the remaining 1 tablespoon of olive oil, over high heat. When the butter begins to brown, add the pieces of chicken, placing them skin-side down into the pan. Be careful not to overcrowd the pan; you will need to cook the chicken in two pans or in two batches. Place the bricks on top of the chicken pieces. It's okay if some chicken sticks out from under the bricks; you can move the bricks around as the chicken cooks.

8. Reduce the heat to medium-high and cook the chicken until it's brown and crispy on one side, for about 8 minutes. Remove the bricks and turn the chicken pieces over. Add the remaining butter pieces to the pan and arrange the bricks on top again. Cook for another 8 to 10 minutes on this side, or until the chicken is just cooked through.

9. Remove the bricks from the pan. When cool, you can remove the first two layers of foil from the bricks and re-wrap them for later use.

10. Place the chicken onto a large platter, skin-side up. Sprinkle each piece generously with za'atar and serve.

VARIATION

You can also use 4 deboned, skin-on chicken breasts and 4 deboned, skin-on chicken thighs for this recipe, preparing them as above. Although you won't be able to create marbled meat, this variation still makes a delicious chicken dish.

Greek Salad with Winter Vegetables, Apple, and Barrel-Aged Feta Cheese

In Greece, the dish that Americans call Greek salad is called "village salad," and it's made with cucumbers, onions, peppers, olives, tomatoes, and feta. Rarely is any lettuce served.

The key to a great Greek salad lies in the feta and the kalamata olives. It's worth going out of your way to find barrel-aged feta; the barrel-aging process makes it firm but creamy with a nice strong flavor. French feta is creamier, and there are many choices, so taste as many as you can and simply choose your favorite. And if you have access to a Greek market, beg them for barrel-aged feta.

You can cook the cauliflower and Brussels sprouts up to a day ahead of time, but the squash is better cooked and eaten the same day.

SERVES 8 AS A FIRST COURSE

- 1 small to medium buttercup squash (about 2 pounds)
- 2 tablespoons olive oil
- 1 tablespoon salt plus more to taste

Pepper to taste

Ice cubes

- ½ head cauliflower, cored and washed

Pinch of baking soda

- 8 Brussels sprouts, outer leaves trimmed and cut in half lengthwise
- 1 bulb fennel, quartered, cored, tough outer layer removed and cut into a ¼- to ½-inch dice
- 1 Granny Smith apple, cored and cut into a ¼- to ½-inch dice
- 16 kalamata olives, pitted
- ½ red onion, peeled and finely chopped
- 2½ tablespoons freshly squeezed lemon juice (about 1 large lemon)
- 4 tablespoons extra-virgin olive oil
- 2 teaspoons dried, sieved oregano (see page 246)
- 1 pound barrel-aged or French feta cheese

1. Preheat the oven to 350°F.

2. Cut the squash in half widthwise and use a small spoon to scoop out the seeds. Slice each half into quarters and then into eighths so that you have 8 wedges of squash. Toss the squash with the 2 tablespoons olive oil on a heavy baking sheet and season well with salt and pepper to taste. Roast the squash in the oven for about 25 minutes, until just tender. Set aside to cool.

3. Prepare a medium bowl of ice water.

4. Bring a 2-quart saucepan of water to a boil over high heat and season with 1 tablespoon of salt.

5. Using a small paring knife or your fingers, break the cauliflower into small florets. Add the cauliflower to the water and boil for 4 minutes, or until it is just tender. Using a slotted spoon, remove the cauliflower from the water and drop it into the ice water. Let it chill for about 3 minutes, drain well, pat dry with paper towels, and set aside.

6. Prepare another medium bowl of ice water.

7. Add a pinch of baking soda to the pot of boiling water and drop the Brussels sprouts in. The baking soda helps keep the Brussels sprouts a nice bright green, but don't add more than a pinch, or they will turn out mushy. Cook them for about 5 minutes, or until they are just tender.

8. Drain the Brussels sprouts and place them in the bowl of ice water to chill for about 5 minutes. Drain well, pat dry with paper towels, and set aside.

9. When the squash is cool enough to handle, remove the skin by placing the wedges skin-side down on a cutting board and running a paring knife between the skin and the squash, staying as close to the skin as possible. Cut the squash into ½-inch chunks and place them in a large mixing bowl. You should have about 1½ cups of diced squash.

10. Cut the cores off the Brussels sprouts and break the leaves up with your fingers. Add the leaves and the cauliflower to the mixing bowl with the squash.

11. Add the fennel and the apple to the rest of the vegetables. Stir to combine them and sprinkle the top with the olives.

12. Prepare the vinaigrette in a small mixing bowl: whisk together the onion, lemon juice, extra-virgin olive oil, and oregano. Season with salt and pepper. Let the mixture sit for at least 5 minutes to lightly pickle the onion (it will turn bright pink) before dressing the salad.

13. Toss the vegetables with the vinaigrette and season the salad with salt and pepper.

14. To serve, cut the feta into 8 equal slices. Spoon the salad into 8 salad bowls and top each salad with a slice of feta.

SIEVING DRIED HERBS

I push my dried herbs through a medium-fine sieve to powder the leaves and remove any bits of stem before I use them. Dried herbs store well in an airtight container in a cool, dark place for a couple of months.

best of the best exclusive

Crispy Za'atar Pinwheels

MAKES ABOUT 3 DOZEN PINWHEELS

1½ cups all-purpose flour, plus more for dusting

½ pound chilled cream cheese, cut into 1-inch pieces

2 sticks cold unsalted butter, cut into ½-inch pieces

¾ teaspoon salt

3 tablespoons za'atar (see Editor's Note, page 240)

1. Line 2 large baking sheets with parchment paper. In a standing mixer fitted with the paddle, beat the 1½ cups of flour with the cream cheese, butter and salt at low speed until the dough just comes together, about 1 minute. Transfer the dough to a lightly floured work surface and knead until smooth. Divide the dough in half and pat each piece into a rectangle.

2. Roll out each piece of dough to a 10-by-18-inch rectangle, about ⅛ inch thick. Sprinkle the za'atar evenly over the dough. Using a rolling pin, gently roll over the za'atar so it adheres to the dough.

3. Working from a long side of each rectangle, very loosely roll up the dough. Trim off the rough ends. Cut the rolls crosswise into ¾-inch-thick slices and arrange on the prepared baking sheets. Refrigerate for 30 minutes or until chilled.

4. Preheat the oven to 400°. Bake the pinwheels for about 25 minutes, until golden brown. Let cool slightly, then serve warm or at room temperature.

MAKE AHEAD The pinwheels can be stored in an airtight container at room temperature for up to 3 days.

Editor's Note

Sortun gives rich, flaky croissants a Lebanese flavor by sprinkling them with za'atar. In this streamlined approach, the same dough is seasoned, rolled into a log and then sliced crosswise to create crisp, addictive spirals.

Simple Roast Chicken, p. 250

Sparks in the Kitchen

By Katy Sparks with Andrea Strong

When Katy Sparks, a *Food & Wine* magazine Best New Chef 1998, had a son, she went from working as a restaurant chef and hardly ever cooking at home to making dinner most nights. In her first cookbook, she shares those everyday recipes, which use surprising herbs and spices. For instance, her version of asparagus vinaigrette includes ginger and chile oil, and her roast chicken is unexpectedly seasoned with coriander. "It adds a nice spicy citrus flavor, but you don't quite know what it is," Sparks says.

Published by Alfred A. Knopf, $30.
Find more recipes by Katy Sparks at foodandwine.com/sparks

Simple Roast Chicken

Before I became a mother, I used to make my husband pretty much fend for himself while I was working five nights a week at a restaurant. All that has changed. I want to make sure Luke and Michael have some good meals together, so I've taken to giving small cooking classes to the two of them when I'm home. By teaching Michael a few of the basics, I feel less guilty about not being around every night to cook a good, healthy meal for Luke— I know his dad can. We've found that a well-seasoned chicken slid into a hot oven becomes, with almost no effort, one of the most satisfying dinners we make. The first trick is to buy a well-raised bird that has been allowed to roam around and build up some muscle and flavor. The so-called free-range birds are good, but locally raised, organic birds are even better. Yes, they are a little more expensive, but the difference in flavor is well worth it.

The next family secret is to make a compound butter; a softened butter blended with flavorings, the combinations and possibilities of which are endless. Another avenue of flavor is cavity "stuffing." This can be as simple as a half a lemon you have in the fridge getting dry or a sprig of herbs or a few mushroom stems—anything that will release some extra flavor and aroma.

The last family secret is my key to knowing when your chicken is done. It may sound silly, but it's true: I know my chicken is done when it smells like chicken—the delicious aroma fills my kitchen. Try it. It's foolproof.

SERVES 4–6

FOR THE LEMON AND HERB COMPOUND BUTTER

  1 stick butter, softened

Zest of 1 lemon (save the naked lemon to stuff into the cavity)

  ½ cup minced herbs—any combination of parsley, tarragon, chervil, cilantro, basil, sage, and rosemary
       (keep the stripped herb stems for the cavity)

  2 cloves garlic, mashed to a paste with 1 teaspoon salt

Freshly ground black pepper

FOR THE CHICKEN

  1 chicken (approximately 4½ pounds)

Salt and pepper

  1 teaspoon freshly ground coriander seed (optional)

FOR THE SAUCE (OPTIONAL)

  1 tablespoon flour

  1 cup chicken stock (use homemade or organic,
      low-sodium boxed), or water

Preheat oven to 400°F.

PREPARE THE COMPOUND BUTTER

In a bowl, beat the softened butter with a spoon until smooth. Stir in
the lemon zest, herbs, garlic, and pepper. Take half of the butter and roll it
into a 1-inch-thick cylinder, wrap in foil, label, and pop it in the freezer
for future use.

CLEAN AND ROAST THE CHICKEN

Rinse the whole bird under cold water and pat dry, inside and out. Season
inside the cavity with salt, pepper, and coriander seed, if using. Place the
bird on your work surface so the cavity is facing you. Slide your forefinger
gently under the skin of the breast to loosen it from the meat. When you have
made a pocket on both sides of the breast, carefully stuff 2 tablespoons of
the compound butter under the skin of each side, pressing it toward the front
as you go. You don't want to tear the skin, so work slowly and gently. Rub
the rest of the butter all over the bird, including the thighs and legs. Season
liberally with salt, pepper, and coriander seed. I keep a separate peppermill
just for coriander seed, which I think works so well with poultry—it has a
fragrance reminiscent of citrus and sage.

Place the bird in a roasting pan that is not much bigger than the bird itself;
you don't want the melting butter to burn, which will happen if there is too
much exposed surface area. I usually use my 9-by-11-inch glass Pyrex dish.

Editor's Note

For the compound
butter, the more intense
herbs—rosemary, sage
and cilantro—work well
when combined with the
milder parsley, tarragon
and basil, but they are
overpowering on their
own. If you use only the
strongly flavored herbs,
reduce the total quantity
to 2 tablespoons.

I find that when I put the bird right in a hot oven with all this butter under the skin there is no need for basting or turning, but you can baste and turn the chicken if you like. I also don't truss the bird for family. It looks less than elegant splayed open, but the hot air circulates nicely around it and crisps the skin in the leg folds as well as the breast. If I am entertaining and want to carve the bird at the table, I truss.

Once the bird is in the hot oven, expect it to take 1 hour and 20 minutes or so. To test, pierce the thickest part of the thigh; if the juices run clear, it's done. Another sign that your bird is done is that the leg joint will be loose and wobbly when you tug on it.

Before carving, it's important to rest the bird on a platter for 10–15 minutes. If you try to carve a hot chicken, you'll let all the juices escape, and the meat will be dry and stringy instead of sleek and moist. Return any juices that accumulate on the platter back to the roasting pan.

At this point you have a few options for saucing the bird. Usually, I just spoon the pan drippings over the chicken for flavor and moisture, but if you want to make a sauce or gravy, you'll need to skim off the fat, leaving 1 or 2 tablespoons behind. Sprinkle the pan juices with a tablespoon of flour, scraping up the brown bits, add maybe a cup or so of water or chicken stock, and bring it up to a boil for a couple of minutes, then strain the sauce through a sieve. Making the gravy this way is really not much trouble and leaves you with a smooth and thickened sauce.

Pan-Roasted Chicken Thighs with Calvados Cream and Onion-Sage Confit

Chicken thighs are often considered the poor cousin to the exalted breast, but they shouldn't be. Particularly when cooked on the bone, they have a rich flavor and juiciness that the leaner breast can only envy. It's fun to use this humble cut and elevate it to a higher status with the help of apple brandy and voluptuous crème fraîche. Calvados is the justly famous brandy from Normandy, and I wouldn't substitute any other apple liquor here. Calvados has a refinement like none other.

SERVES 4–6

FOR THE CHICKEN

8 to 12 chicken thighs, bone-in

Salt and pepper

1   teaspoon freshly ground coriander seed (optional)

2   tablespoons butter

FOR THE CALVADOS CREAM SAUCE

1   shallot, thinly sliced

1   tablespoon minced fresh lemongrass root (optional)

6 to 8 small crimini or white mushrooms, brushed clean and sliced

½   cup Calvados

½   cup dry hard cider or regular sweet cider

½   cup chicken stock

⅓   cup crème fraîche or heavy cream

Salt and pepper

Freshly grated nutmeg

Onion-Sage Confit (recipe follows)

PREPARE THE CHICKEN

Rinse the chicken under cold water and pat dry with paper towels. Season well with salt, pepper, and coriander if using. Find a large skillet that will accommodate the thighs with at least ¼ inch of room between them—but not too much extra space, either. Use 2 pans if necessary. Melt the butter

Editor's Note

Both the Pan-Roasted Chicken Thighs and the Onion-Sage Confit are great recipes to have in your repertoire, and you don't need to serve them together. The chicken thighs, with their refined, creamy sauce, are elegant on their own, while the confit is a spectacular way to dress up chicken breasts or pork.

over medium-high heat and brown the thighs on both sides; this will take about 8 minutes. Transfer the thighs to a plate while making the sauce. Reserve the fat in the pan.

MAKE THE CALVADOS CREAM SAUCE

Using the butter and chicken fat that remains in the pan, sauté the shallots, lemongrass (if using), and mushrooms until tender, about 2 minutes. Pull the pan away from the heat before pouring in the Calvados. You don't want to get the bottle of Calvados anywhere near an open flame. This is a high-proof alcohol and will ignite easily—not a problem when it happens in the pan, but a big problem when it happens in your hand. Measure out what you need and pour it in gently off the heat, then return the pan to the stovetop. When the alcohol is warm enough, it may spontaneously ignite, but this is fine, just let it burn off. If it doesn't ignite, it will burn off by boiling down.

Pour in the cider and chicken stock and whisk in the crème fraîche. Return the chicken to the pan and reduce heat to a simmer. Lightly tent the pan with foil, which will allow some evaporation to thicken the sauce but will trap enough heat in the pan so the chicken can cook evenly.

Simmer the chicken for 15–20 minutes. When you think it's ready, pull out a thigh and pierce it in the thickest part. If the juices run clear, it's done. Remove all the thighs and reduce the sauce a bit more, until it lightly coats a spoon. Season with salt, pepper, and nutmeg, to taste. Serve the chicken with the sauce spooned over it and some warm Onion-Sage Confit.

Onion-Sage Confit

Onions are naturally sweet, and slow cooking only accentuates this trait. I love to add the sage early in their cooking so it really permeates the whole dish. Thyme is also nice, and in that case I would omit the cider vinegar and replace it with about a quarter cup of diced, briny black olives or oil-cured olives.

MAKES APPROXIMATELY 1½ CUPS

- 2 tablespoons olive oil
- 1 tablespoon butter
- 2 large onions, sliced thin
- 8 to 10 sage leaves, cut into ¼-inch ribbons
- 1 tablespoon cider vinegar or sherry vinegar
- 2 tablespoons dried currants (optional)

Salt and freshly ground black pepper

Heat the olive oil and butter together in a heavy skillet over medium heat. Stir in the onions and coat them well with the oil and butter, add the sage, and cook over medium-low heat while stirring occasionally for 25–30 minutes, or until the onions are deeply browned and very soft. Sprinkle the vinegar over the onions and add the dried currants, if desired. Season lightly with salt and pepper. You don't want this too salty—it gets in the way of the lovely sweet flavor—but lots of pepper is divine!

Asparagus Vinaigrette with Lemon-Pistachio Dressing and Manchego Cheese

Sparks on Peeling Ginger

A lot of chefs use a spoon to peel fresh ginger, and that works really well if the ginger is very tender and young, with thin, tight, glossy skin. For older ginger I use a paring knife, first breaking the ginger apart so I don't have to cut around big, irregular knobs. I store unpeeled ginger in the fridge in sandwich bags.

SERVES 6

- 1 shallot, minced
- 2 teaspoons minced fresh ginger
- Pinch of salt
- Juice of 1 lemon
- ⅓ cup extra-virgin olive oil
- Salt and pepper
- 1½ pounds local asparagus, cooked (see Note)
- ¼ pound Manchego cheese, or aged goat cheese or Pecorino Romano, sliced thin
- ½ cup toasted pistachios, from Turkey or California
- 2 to 3 tablespoons Red Chile Oil (recipe follows; optional)

Put the shallot and the ginger in a medium bowl and sprinkle them with the salt. Drizzle in the lemon juice and olive oil and whisk well. Taste for seasoning, adding salt and pepper as you see fit.

To serve, divide the chilled asparagus among 6 plates, or set them up on a decorative platter, with all the spears aligned. Season with salt and pepper, drizzle on the vinaigrette, and top with thin slices of Manchego cheese. (A great trick is to use a vegetable peeler for the cheese—you get thin shavings in a flash.) Scatter some toasted pistachios on top and garnish with a little red chile oil, if desired.

NOTE There are many schools of thought on how to cook asparagus. Some cooks steam the spears standing up, some quench them in lots of boiling, salted water. I find that cooking asparagus lying down in a shallow amount of well-salted water works the best. (I also like to choose asparagus that are on the fatter side—more middle and less peel.) This method conserves as much asparagus flavor as possible and allows you to test for doneness easily by poking a stalk with the tip of a sharp knife—when the knife slides out effortlessly, the asparagus is done. I don't believe in "al dente" asparagus— I find that the flavor doesn't fully develop until they are cooked until just tender. I avoid "shocking" the asparagus in ice water, which can damage the texture. Instead, I lay them out single file on plates, and pop them in the fridge or freezer for a few minutes. (Just don't forget they're in the freezer!)

Red Chile Oil

My favorite red chile of all is the ancho. It is a ripened and dried poblano chile that is sold both as a whole pod and as a roasted and ground powder. (The pods should be soaked in hot water until soft, and then the flesh can be scraped from the skins. The flesh is a gorgeous deep-red color and is used to thicken and flavor chiles, stews, and sauces.) More often, though, I use it in its powdered form. Ancho is more sweet than hot since the ripening and drying create a raisin-like flavor. The powder will easily bleed its lovely color into whatever you're cooking and has mild thickening properties as well when whisked into a vinaigrette or sauce. Once made into this flavored oil, you can drizzle it over any dish that could use a little splash of color and mild heat.

MAKES APPROXIMATELY 1 CUP

- 2 cloves garlic
- 1 tablespoon olive oil
- ¼ cup ancho chile powder
- 1 cup canola oil
- 1 teaspoon salt

In a small pan, sauté the whole cloves of garlic in the olive oil until they are golden brown and tender. Cover the pan while sautéing the garlic to trap the steam and keep it from burning. Transfer the garlic and any oil from the pan to a blender. Add the ancho powder, canola oil, and salt and run on low speed for 5 full minutes. This is necessary to really suspend the chile in the oil so it can develop its full flavor. Pour the contents of the blender into a coffee filter or a double layer of cheesecloth suspended over a cup. The oil should drip out slowly over the course of several hours. Don't press on the solids or the oil will be cloudy. You can keep the oil in the fridge for up to 2 weeks.

Editor's Note
Start the Red Chile Oil a few hours in advance since it needs time to drip through the cheesecloth. If you prefer, you can substitute Italian chile-infused olive oil or omit it entirely; the asparagus will still be incredible.

Shrimp and Zucchini Salad with Red Curry Sauce

Editor's Note

Simmer vegetables or chicken in this creamy, fragrant red curry sauce to serve over rice, or dilute it with stock to use as a base for curried soup, adding noodles and seafood, meat or poultry.

4 SERVINGS

¼ cup salted roasted cashews

¼ cup vegetable oil

1 small poblano chile, seeded and finely diced

1 small onion, finely diced

2 garlic cloves, minced

2 tablespoons finely grated fresh ginger

½ cup dry white wine

1½ cups unsweetened coconut milk (12 ounces)

2 tablespoons Thai red curry paste

1 roasted red bell pepper from a jar, cut into ½-inch dice

Juice and finely grated zest of 1 lime

Kosher salt and freshly ground pepper

2 tablespoons unsalted butter

4 medium zucchini (1½ pounds), very thinly sliced lengthwise with a vegetable peeler or on a mandoline

1 pound large shrimp, shelled and deveined

2 teaspoons chopped cilantro

1. Preheat the oven to 350°. In a pie plate, toast the cashews for 8 minutes, or until fragrant. Let cool, then coarsely chop.

2. In a large saucepan, heat 2 tablespoons of the vegetable oil. Add the poblano, onion, garlic and ginger and cook over moderately high heat until the onion is softened, about 5 minutes. Add the wine and cook until the pan is almost dry, about 1 minute. Add the coconut milk, red curry paste and roasted red pepper and simmer over low heat, stirring occasionally, until the sauce is slightly thickened, about 10 minutes.

3. Transfer the curry sauce to a blender and puree until smooth. Add the lime juice and zest and season with salt and pepper. Return the sauce to the saucepan and keep warm.

4. In a large skillet, melt the butter. Add the zucchini, season with salt and cook over moderate heat, tossing, until just tender, about 4 minutes. Transfer the zucchini to a platter.

5. In the same skillet, heat the remaining 2 tablespoons of vegetable oil. Season the shrimp with salt and pepper. Add the shrimp to the skillet and cook over moderately high heat until opaque throughout, about 4 minutes. Top the zucchini with the shrimp. Spoon some of the curry sauce over and around the shrimp and zucchini, sprinkle with the cashews and cilantro and serve.

MAKE AHEAD The curry sauce can be refrigerated for up to 4 days.

Roasted Veal Chops
with Honey, p. 262

Cucina of Le Marche

By Fabio Trabocchi with Peter Kaminsky

"Everyone knows Tuscany, Rome and Venice, but Le Marche is an overlooked area in Italy," says Fabio Trabocchi, a *Food & Wine* magazine Best New Chef 2002, explaining why he wrote a cookbook on his native region, which is isolated from the rest of the country by the Apennine Mountains. Trabocchi has a quirky sense of humor: For instance, he describes how his Beef Tenderloin with Fondue of Talamello Cheese was inspired by a Philly cheesesteak. And all of his recipes, like Farro Soup with Pecorino and Prosciutto, are deliciously satisfying.

Published by Ecco, $32.50.
Find more recipes by Fabio Trabocchi at foodandwine.com/trabocchi

Roasted Veal Chops with Honey

Cotoletta di Vitello al Miele

We always bought our veal—delicate in texture but deep and rich in taste—from Nello Salvucci, our favorite butcher. Like so many of our friends, he was another transplant from the farm in Santo Stefano. I loved going to see him after the Thursday market in town, and as I grew older, I used to hang around his shop asking questions about meat. Nello gave me a big education; all about butchering, deboning, and the ins and outs of meat.

The sauce for this veal dish is made with grapes and honey (in the old days, families like ours would have used honey as a sweetener instead of the more costly cane sugar). One of my favorites is Corbezzolo honey, made from the nectar of the arbutus shrub—also called strawberry tree—whose flowers can be seen all over the countryside of Le Marche and Piemonte. In addition to the sweetness, it has a bitter note that works almost as a palate refresher.

SERVES 6

6 veal rib chops, about 8 ounces each and 1 inch thick

Kosher salt and freshly ground black pepper

¾ pound seedless green grapes

4 tablespoons (2 ounces) unsalted butter, plus 4 tablespoons (2 ounces) cold unsalted butter

8 whole cloves

2 bay leaves, preferably fresh

2 sprigs sage

4 oil-packed anchovy fillets, chopped

2 cups dry white wine, such as Verdicchio or Pinot Grigio

1½ cups Chicken Stock (page 266)

2 tablespoons Corbezzolo honey or other aromatic honey

Season the veal chops lightly with salt and pepper. Place on a plate, cover, and let rest for 30 minutes.

Slice the grapes lengthwise in half. Set aside.

Place two large sauté pans over medium-high heat. Melt 2 tablespoons of the butter in each pan. Add 3 chops to each pan and brown them for about 3 minutes on each side. Add half of the cloves, bay leaves, sage, and anchovies to each pan. Sauté for 3 minutes.

Add 1 cup of wine to each pan and bring to a boil, scraping the browned bits from the bottom with a wooden spatula or spoon. Cook until the wine has almost completely evaporated.

Turn the chops and add ¾ cup of the chicken stock to each pan. Bring to a simmer and cook the veal for 4 minutes. Turn the veal over and simmer for an additional 4 minutes, or until cooked to medium. Transfer the veal to a serving dish and cover with aluminum foil to keep warm.

Pour the cooking liquid from both pans through a fine-mesh strainer into a saucepan. Bring to a boil, then reduce the heat and simmer for 5 minutes. Add the grapes and honey, stir, and cook for 4 minutes.

Stir the remaining 4 tablespoons cold butter bit by bit into the sauce. Season to taste with salt and pepper. Spoon the sauce over the veal chops and serve.

Farro Soup with Pecorino and Prosciutto

Minestra all'Antica

Trabocchi on Variations

This is the kind of soup that shepherds would eat. It's like a meal in a bowl, with all the nutrients you need to keep you going. You can vary the soup by serving it topped with a sunny-side-up fried egg, using Parmesan cheese instead of pecorino or, if you're feeling rich, adding some sliced truffle.

Italians have been eating farro for thousands of years, and this is a classic Le Marche soup. However, I never knew much about this hearty and delicious grain until I worked in the kitchen of Silvano Pettinari, one of my teachers in culinary school. He had a restaurant in the old walled city of Corinaldo.

People from my part of Le Marche often say that the people from Corinaldo are crazy. "It's the winds," is the way the old grandmothers explain things. The following story is typical: A man named Signore Persiano (his name means "shutters") received regular payments from his son in America to build a home in Corinaldo so that the son could one day return there after making his fortune in the New World. Every time the son wrote home, the father assured him that everything was going fine, when in fact all of the son's money was being spent on wine. Finally, though, the son asked to see a picture of his dream house and the father, in desperate straits, had a façade constructed, complete with window boxes and flowers. Standing on a ladder, he leaned out the window and posed for a picture of himself waving happily from the window. He sent the photo off to his son—and the façade still stands to this day.

Choose a young pecorino cheese for this. It will be milder than aged pecorino, as well as easier to chop.

SERVES 6

¼ cup plus 2 tablespoons extra-virgin olive oil, plus more for drizzling

1¼ cups diced (¼-inch) celery

1 cup diced onions

¾ cup diced (¼-inch) prosciutto

1¾ cups farro or barley

2 quarts Chicken Stock (recipe follows), warmed

Kosher salt and freshly ground black pepper

Six ½-inch-thick slices crusty country bread, such as ciabatta

¾ cup coarsely chopped mild pecorino

3 tablespoons chopped marjoram

In a medium saucepan, heat ¼ cup of the olive oil over medium heat. Add the celery, onions, and prosciutto and cook until the vegetables are soft and translucent. Add the farro and warm chicken stock and quickly bring to a simmer. Cover, reduce the heat to low, and cook for 45 minutes to 1 hour, or until the farro is tender. Remove the soup from the heat and season to taste with salt and pepper.

Meanwhile, brush the bread on both sides with the remaining 2 tablespoons olive oil. Grill or toast (you can use a ridged cast-iron grill pan) until golden brown on both sides.

Place 1 slice of grilled bread in the bottom of each soup bowl. Top the bread with the pecorino and marjoram. Ladle in the hot soup and garnish each bowl with a drizzle of olive oil. Serve immediately.

Chicken Stock

MAKES 7 QUARTS

- 2 chickens
- 1 pound chicken necks (optional)
- ½ pound cleaned chicken feet (optional)
- Pinch of kosher salt
- 3½ quarts cold water
- 3½ quarts ice cubes
- 3 stalks celery
- 2 medium carrots
- 2 medium onions, skin left on, cut in half
- 1 small bouquet garni—thyme sprigs, Italian parsley stems, and bay leaves
- 1 tablespoon crushed white peppercorns

Rinse the chickens well, making sure to remove any visible blood. If using, rinse the necks and/or feet well.

Place the chickens, and necks and/or feet, in a large stockpot. Add the salt and water and slowly bring to a simmer over medium heat, skimming well to remove all the impurities that rise to the top.

Add the ice cubes, then skim the fat and any additional impurities that form on the surface. When the liquid returns to a simmer, add the celery, carrots, onions, bouquet garni, and peppercorns. Simmer for about 2 hours longer, skimming frequently.

Remove from the stove and let the stock stand for at least 30 minutes.

Set a fine strainer over a large container and ladle the stock into the strainer. Discard the liquid at the very bottom of the pot, since this is likely to contain impurities.

To cool the stock quickly, set the container in ice (fill up your sink with ice water to do this).

Refrigerate for up to 48 hours, or transfer to smaller containers and freeze.

Beef Tenderloin with Fondue of Talamello Cheese

Filetto all'Ambra di Talamello

Editor's Note

Instead of adding truffles, you can use a soft truffled cheese (like a truffled pecorino), which will impart some of the same aroma.

Recently *Food & Wine* magazine asked me for some recipes inspired by Le Marche. Because America is a beef-loving country, I thought I'd dream up something I could make with our amazing beef cattle called razza marchigiana (they are related to the giant Tuscan Chianina—and, in my opinion, better). Then I thought of the Philadelphia cheesesteak, which surprised me the first time I had it: I was expecting a sirloin with cheese on it. This, then, is my marchigiani homage to the cheesesteak—hopefully a bit more refined than the original.

SERVES 6

- 6 beef tenderloin steaks, about 8 ounces each and ¾ inch thick
- Kosher salt and freshly ground white pepper
- 5 tablespoons extra-virgin olive oil
- 6 slices Ambra di Talamello cheese or Italian Fontina or Taleggio, about 3 inches x 3 inches and ⅛ inch thick
- 2 ounces black truffles, shaved or thinly sliced (optional)

Prepare a charcoal fire or preheat a gas grill. Or preheat a cast-iron grill pan over high heat.

Twenty to 30 minutes before grilling, remove the beef from the refrigerator and season lightly with salt and pepper. Put on a plate, cover, and set aside.

Just before grilling, brush each steak generously with olive oil. Grill the beef over medium-high heat for 3 to 4 minutes per side, for medium-rare. One minute before the tenderloins are done, place a slice of cheese on each and cover the grill or pan to allow the cheese to soften (just like on a cheeseburger). Transfer to a plate and let rest in a warm spot for 5 minutes.

Top each steak with slices of truffle, if using, and serve.

Cucina of
Le Marche
*By Fabio Trabocchi
with Peter Kaminsky*

best of the best exclusive

Spanish Tortilla with Mushroom and Basil Salad

6 SERVINGS

¼ cup plus 3 tablespoons extra-virgin olive oil

1 pound potatoes, peeled and cut into ½-inch dice

1 small onion, finely chopped

1 garlic clove, crushed

Kosher salt and freshly ground pepper

8 large eggs

½ pound cremini mushrooms, stems trimmed, caps very thinly sliced

½ cup small basil leaves (about 30 leaves)

1. Preheat the oven to 350°. In a medium nonstick, ovenproof skillet, heat ¼ cup of the olive oil. When the oil is hot, add the potatoes and cook over moderate heat, stirring occasionally, until almost tender, about 12 minutes. Add the onion and garlic, season with salt and pepper and cook until the onion is translucent and the potatoes are cooked through, about 6 minutes. Discard the garlic clove.

2. In a medium bowl, beat the eggs with ½ teaspoon of salt. Pour the eggs over the potatoes and cook until they begin to set around the edge, about 30 seconds. Using a spatula, lift the edge of the *tortilla* and tilt the pan, allowing the uncooked eggs to seep underneath. Cook until the bottom is set, about 3 minutes longer. Transfer the skillet to the oven and bake for about 7 minutes, until the *tortilla* is just set in the center.

3. Meanwhile, in a medium bowl, toss the mushrooms with the basil leaves and the remaining 3 tablespoons of olive oil; season with salt and pepper. Slide the *tortilla* onto a platter, cut into wedges and serve with the mushroom salad.

MAKE AHEAD The *tortilla* can be made up to 2 hours ahead and served at room temperature.

Editor's Note

Trabocchi's wife is from the Spanish island of Mallorca, and she has been cooking versions of this comforting potato-and-egg dish for him since they met. Here Trabocchi puts an Italian spin on it by adding fresh basil.

Pistou Soup, p. 272

The Food of France

By Sarah Woodward

"The supposed demise of French food has been much written about in recent years," Sarah Woodward notes. But in her cookbook, this English food and travel writer makes the case that France's regional cooking traditions are very much alive. Each chapter opens with an essay on an area in France—Normandy, Provence—followed by a dozen of its traditional recipes. The emphasis is on approachability. Instead of providing a complicated recipe for bouillabaisse, for instance, Woodward says, "Keep it simple: Go to a restaurant in Marseille."

Published by Kyle Books, $29.95.

Pistou Soup
Soupe au Pistou

Woodward on Substitutions

If you don't have nice Swiss chard for this recipe, don't worry about trying to substitute something else. I don't think people should follow recipes too rigidly. As a general rule, if you can't get an ingredient, just leave it out.

Italy has pesto and Provence has pistou. There is lively debate as to who had it first, but the difference is clear: there are no pine nuts in the French version. But, just as in Italy, you will find pistou spooned over pasta and stirred into soups. I hardly dare to write it, but soupe au pistou is remarkably like a minestrone. It is at its best made in late spring, when the vegetables and the basil are at their sweetest.

SERVES 4 TO 6

- 2 small young leeks
- 5 fat garlic cloves
- Extra virgin olive oil
- 6 plum tomatoes
- Salt
- White sugar
- Tops of several leaves of Swiss chard, if available, shredded
- ½ pound green beans, topped, tailed and cut into bite-sized lengths
- Bouquet garni of parsley, sage and basil
- 2 medium-sized zucchini, diced
- 1 cup cooked borlotti or white haricot beans
- A good bunch of fresh basil
- A good hunk (around ⅓ pound) of fresh Parmesan, shredded
- ¼ pound vermicelli

Finely chop the white part of the leeks, discarding the green tops. Peel 2 of the garlic cloves and chop finely. Heat 2 tablespoons oil in a large heavy pan big enough to make the soup in. Add the leeks and chopped garlic and sweat gently for 10 minutes, stirring occasionally. It is important that the leeks and garlic do not brown.

While they are cooking, pour boiling water over the tomatoes, leave for 45 seconds, then remove and peel as soon as they are cool enough to handle. Cut in half, remove the seeds and roughly dice the flesh. (In almost all other instances I would use canned tomatoes, but for this soup, which relies on fresh ingredients, this really is a necessary step.)

Add the tomatoes to the leek and garlic mix, together with a good pinch each of salt and sugar. Cook, stirring several times, until the tomatoes have begun to break down, 5 minutes. Remove from the heat.

Bring 1¼ quarts lightly salted water to the boil and blanch the Swiss chard tops, if you have them, for 1 minute. Lift out with a slotted spoon and then cook the green beans in the same liquor with the bouquet garni for 2 minutes. Add the liquor, green beans, bouquet garni, Swiss chard tops, diced zucchini and borlotti or haricot beans to the leek and tomato mixture, bring back to the boil and reduce to a simmer.

Cook for 10 minutes, during which time you can make the pistou. Traditionally this is done in a pestle and mortar but a food processor does perfectly well, as long as you remember the sauce should be quite chunky. Crush the remaining garlic cloves with a generous pinch of salt then whiz in the basil leaves, stripped from the stalk, and the Parmesan. Drizzle in just enough oil to make an emulsion—6 tablespoons as an estimate.

Bring the soup back to the boil and add the vermicelli. Cook for 5 minutes, until the pasta is just cooked. Remove from the heat, check seasoning, and leave to cool for 10 minutes before stirring in the pistou. A sprinkle of Parmesan and a few basil leaves floating in the soup do no harm.

Woodward on Sugar

Not everyone adds sugar to pistou soup, but I use a little pinch unless I've got really great tomatoes. If I were making this in Provence, where the tomatoes are very sweet, I would leave out the sugar.

Cherry Pudding
Clafoutis aux Cerises

The cherries arrive late in this hilly region but driving through in the spring the blossom is stunning. And when the cherries do come (or when they are imported from nearby Limousin) the favorite way to treat them is in a clafoutis, a baked sweet batter pudding that the locals fondly describe as a 'taste of childhood.' Ideally the cherries should be left unpitted so that they keep their texture.

SERVES 6

Generous 1 cup whole milk

1½ pound cherries

1½ cups all-purpose flour

½ cup superfine sugar

A pinch of salt

  4 tablespoons unsalted butter

  4 large eggs, beaten well

Bring the milk to the boil, taking care that it does not boil over. As soon as it starts to fizz up, take it off the heat and leave to cool slightly. Remove the skin. Preheat the oven to 350°F.

Butter a deep ovenproof dish liberally and scatter the cherries over the base, making sure they are evenly distributed. Sift the flour with the sugar and salt into a mixing bowl. Melt the butter and remove any scum. Make a well in the center of the flour and whisk in the beaten eggs, then, very slowly, the melted butter, followed by the milk, which should still be warm. Whisk thoroughly so that you have a smooth batter and pour over the cherries.

Bake until the batter rises and the top browns, 40–45 minutes. Leave the oven door slightly open for the last 5 minutes of cooking, so that the batter doesn't sink the minute you take it out of the heat. Serve straight away, sprinkled with confectioners' sugar if you like.

Eggs Poached in Red Wine
Oeufs en Meurette

Woodward on Red Wine

Typically a Pinot Noir would be used here, since the Burgundians have it flowing out of their ears, but any good quality, fruity *vin de pays* will do the trick. You will want something you can drink with the dish—it makes the sauce better, and what else would you do with the rest of the bottle?

One night a wine grower found nothing in the larder but eggs, bacon, butter and, of course, bread and red wine. So he decided to cook them all together; or so legend has it. But whatever its origin, this simple yet luxurious dish has become a Burgundian classic. In restaurants, it is usually offered as a starter, but accompanied by a simple green salad it also makes a splendid supper.

SERVES 2

- 3 tablespoons unsalted butter
- ¼ pound smoked bacon in lardons
- 4 pink shallots, peeled and finely chopped
- 2 cups red wine
- 2 tablespoons white wine vinegar
- 4 slices of French bread

Freshly ground black pepper

- 4 fresh eggs, preferably free-range

In a heavy Dutch oven, melt half the butter together with the bacon and cook for 5 minutes. Chop the remaining butter into small pieces and chill in the refrigerator. Add the shallots and cook, stirring regularly, until they are very soft, 15 minutes. Pour in the wine and allow to bubble gently, uncovered, until the sauce is reduced by half, 30 minutes.

Meanwhile, add the white wine vinegar to a pan of water and bring to a rolling boil. Toast the bread on both sides and place in two deep bowls.

Check the seasoning of the sauce (you may like to add some pepper at this stage but generally the bacon provides sufficient salt). Carefully poach the eggs by simply breaking them two at a time into the water; provided they are sufficiently fresh the white will coagulate around the yolk and the cooking time will be a matter of a minute or two. Lift the eggs out with a slotted spoon, making sure all the water has drained off, and place each egg on a slice of the toast. Remove the hot sauce from the heat and quickly swirl in the pieces of butter—this gives the sauce a gloss. Pour over the poached eggs and serve immediately.

best of the best exclusive
Spicy Indian-Style Scrambled Eggs

2 SERVINGS

4 large eggs

¼ teaspoon ground cumin

Pinch of turmeric

Kosher salt

1 tablespoon vegetable oil

1 small red onion, cut into ¼-inch dice

1 small hot red or green chile, seeded and minced

1 garlic clove, minced

1½ teaspoons minced fresh ginger

1 tomato—halved, seeded and cut into ¼-inch dice

Pinch of sugar

2 teaspoons chopped cilantro

Roti (see Note) or toast, for serving

In a medium bowl, whisk the eggs with the cumin, turmeric and ½ teaspoon of salt. In a medium nonstick skillet, heat the oil. Add the onion, chile, garlic and ginger and cook over high heat until the onion just begins to brown, about 3 minutes. Add the tomato, season with salt and the sugar and cook for 1 minute. Reduce the heat to moderately low and pour in the eggs. Cook, stirring constantly, until the eggs are just set, about 1 minute. Fold in the cilantro and serve with roti or toast.

NOTE Roti is a type of unleavened Indian flatbread.

Editor's Note

Woodward says she first had this recipe at a game lodge in southern India, and it has since become her go-to dish when she returns home from a trip. Soothing yet spicy, and perfect for any time of day, it's an ideal antidote to the rich restaurant food she usually eats when she's researching a cookbook.

Credits

The New Greek Cuisine

Braise

A Journey Through International Cuisine

The Cake Book

The Red Cat Cookbook

125 Recipes from New York City's Favorite Neighborhood Restaurant

Heirloom Baking with the Brass Sisters

More Than 100 Years of Recipes Discovered from Family Cookbooks, Original Journals, Scraps of Paper, & Grandmother's Kitchen

Biba's Italy

Favorite Recipes from the Splendid Cities

The Food of Northern Spain

Recipes From the Gastronomic Heartland of Spain

Giada's Family Dinners

How to Boil Water

Life Beyond Takeout

Barefoot Contessa at Home

Everyday Recipes You'll Make Over and Over Again

A Ligurian Kitchen

Recipes and Tales from the Italian Riviera

On Top of Spaghetti...

Macaroni, Linguine, Penne, and Pasta of Every Kind

Stonewall Kitchen Favorites

Delicious Recipes to Share with Family and Friends Every Day

The Lee Bros. Southern Cookbook
Stories and Recipes for Southerners and Would-Be Southerners

"Clover Peach Pies," "Crispy Fried Okra," "Pepper Vinegar," "Sweet Pie Crust," "Sweet Potato Buttermilk Pie." Copyright © 2006 by Martens Maxwell, Inc. "Photograph of Crispy Fried Okra and Sweet Potato Buttermilk Pie." Copyright © 2006 by Gentl & Hayers. From *The Lee Brothers Southern Cookbook: Stories and Recipes for Southerners and Would-Be Southerners* by Matt Lee and Ted Lee. Used by permission of W. W. Norton & Company, Inc.

Lobel's Meat and Wine
Great Recipes for Cooking and Pairing

From *Lobel's Meat and Wine* by Stanley, Leon, Evan, Mark and David Lobel with Mary Goodbody and David Whiteman. Text copyright © 2006 by Morris Lobel and Sons Inc. Photographs copyright © 2006 by James Baigrie. Published by Chronicle Books LLC.

Jamie's Italy

Excerpted from *Jamie's Italy* by Jamie Oliver. Copyright © 2006 Jamie Oliver. All rights reserved. Published by Hyperion. (Available wherever books are sold.) Photographs copyright © 2006 David Loftus. Additional photographs copyright © 2006 Christ Terry and Peter Begg.

Big Small Plates

Reprinted with permission from *Big Small Plates* by Cindy Pawlcyn. Copyright © 2006 by Cindy Pawlcyn, Photography copyright © 2006 by Laurie Smith and © 2005 Heidi Swanson, Ten Speed Press, Berkeley, CA. www.tenspeed.com.

The Good Home Cookbook
More Than 1,000 Classic American Recipes

From *The Good Home Cookbook* edited by Richard J. Perry. Copyright © 2006 Richard J. Perry. Published by Collectors Press.

The Essence of Chocolate
Recipes for Baking and Cooking with Fine Chocolate

Excerpted from *The Essence of Chocolate* by John Scharffenberger and Robert Steinberg. Copyright © 2006 Scharffen Berger Chocolate Maker, Inc. Photographs copyright © 2005 Deborah Jones. Reprinted by permission of Hyperion. All rights reserved. Available wherever books are sold.

¡Baja! Cooking on the Edge

Reprinted from: *¡Baja! Cooking on the Edge* by Deborah M. Schneider. Copyright © 2006 by Deborah M. Schneider. Photographs © 2006 by Maren Caruso. Permission granted by Rodale, Inc., Emmaus, PA 18098. Available wherever books are sold or directly from the publisher by calling (800) 848-4735 or visit its website at www.rodalestore.com.

The Kitchen Diaries
A Year in the Kitchen with Nigel Slater

"Chicken with Mushrooms and Lemongrass," "Orecchiette with Roast Tomato and Basil Sauce," "Cannellini Beans with Coppa, Spinach and Mustard," "Pumpkin and Tomato Laksa," "Jacket" by Jaya Miceli, design, and Jonathan Lovekin, photograph, from *The Kitchen Diaries* by Nigel Slater and Jonathan Lovekin, Photographs, copyright © 2006 by Nigel Slater. Used by permission of Gotham Books, an imprint of Penguin Group (USA) Inc. Reprinted by permission of HarperCollins Publishers Ltd. © Nigel Slater 2006.

Spice
Flavors of the Eastern Mediterranean

From *Spice* by Ana Sortun. Copyright © 2006 by Ana Sortun. Reprinted by permission of HarperCollins Publishers.

Sparks in the Kitchen

From *Sparks in the Kitchen* by Katy Sparks with Andrea Strong. Photographs by Quentin Bacon, copyright © 2006 by Katy Sparks with Andrea Strong. Used by permission of Alfred A. Knopf, a division of Random House, Inc.

Cucina of Le Marche
A Chef's Treasury of Recipes from Italy's Last Culinary Frontier

From *Cucina of Le Marche* by Fabio Trabocchi and Peter Kaminsky. Copyright © 2006 by Fabio Trabocchi. Photographs copyright © 2006 by Thomas Schauer except on the following pages: i (© Photocuisine/Corbis), 3, 4, 5, 11, 13, 33, 55, 89, 127, 145, 177, 209, 219. Reprinted by permission of HarperCollins Publishers. Ecco.

The Food of France
A Regional Celebration

From *The Food of France* by Sarah Woodward. Copyright © 2006 by Sarah Woodward. Food photography © 2006 Richard Jung. Published by Kyle Books, an imprint of Kyle Cathie Limited.

Index

Page numbers in **bold** indicate photographs.

Index

Page numbers in **bold** indicate photographs.

Index

Page numbers in **bold** indicate photographs.

Index

Page numbers in **bold** indicate photographs.